Skipper's Safe Boating Course

M O S B Y

A Times Mirror
Company

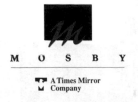

M O S B Y

A Times Mirror Company

Publisher: David Dusthimer
Executive Editor: Richard Weimer
Editors: Eric Duchinsky, Lesley Aaron
Editorial Project Supervisors: Lisa Esposito, Lisa Benson
Project Manager: Christopher J. Baumle
Senior Production Editor: David Orzechowski
Manufacturing Supervisor: Andrew Christensen

If boater safety education is mandatory in your state, check with your state boating law administrator to make sure that the Skipper's Course meets all necessary requirements.

Printed in the United States of America
Composition by Color Associates
Printing/binding by Courier Kendallville, Inc.

Mosby-Year Book, Inc.
11830 Westline Industrial Drive
St. Louis, Missouri 63146

97 98 99 00 / 9 8 7 6 5 4 3 2

ACKNOWLEDGEMENTS & CREDITS

The U.S. Coast Guard would like to acknowledge the following individuals and organizations who were of particular assistance in checking facts, providing technical information and advice, and in many other ways:

John E. Bishop, Waverly, TN

John L. Hunsucker, Ph.D., Houston, TX

William "Jack" Lucey, Fairhope, AL

Neill Miller, Miami, FL

Raymond Miller, Boise, ID

Thomas D. Miller, Miami, FL

Lewis R. Sayre, Miami, FL

American Red Cross, National Headquarters, Washington, DC

U.S. Coast Guard Auxiliary, Headquarters, Washington, DC

U.S. Coast Guard, Boating Education Branch, Headquarters, Washington, DC

Special thanks go to Sharon Scott, Editor, Associate Professor, Danville Community College, Danville, VA; Keri E. Caffrey, illustration/graphic design, Marketing Resource Group (MRG), Winter Park, FL; Mitchell Systems Corporation, Arlington, VA; and Dale A. Currier, MS Ed., Oswego, NY.

Contents approved by the National Association of State Boating Law Administrators and recognized by the U.S. Coast Guard as acceptable to the National Recreational Boating Safety Program

TABLE OF CONTENTS

SKIPPER'S SAFE BOATING COURSE

PREFACE

Recreational boating has undergone enormous growth over the past several years. It is estimated more than 70 million people participate in boating activities each year. Our waterways are becoming increasingly more crowded, and skippers who are careless or ignorant of safe operating procedures and the Navigation Rules are a danger to themselves and other boaters. Boating remains a major cause of transportation fatalities.

This book is designed to help you become a safer boater, and make boating more enjoyable for you. If you are new to boating, the information covered in this course is enough to "whet-your-appetite" for boating. For those who have "skippered" or been boating before, the information in this course will serve as an excellent review.

The book consists of a variety of topics, but is aimed primarily at the needs of the power boater. This book will cover the following information:

- Navigation Rules and safe operating procedures

- Stability and handling characteristics of the boat you are using

- Equipment on the boat and how to use it

- Safety devices and emergency equipment

- Emergency procedures (first aid, etc.)

- Waters you will be using; the tides, currents, and hazards

- Weather conditions

- Your personal limitations and responsibilities

- Boating laws and regulations

- Any licenses and fees for which you are responsible

The course design and self-instructional nature of the units provide you with the flexibility to emphasize course components to meet your specific needs. This course will not make you an "expert" boater, but will give you an understanding of some of the basic terms, requirements and safety procedures needed to be a "safe" boater. Remember, the information presented in this book assumes IDEAL BOATING CONDITIONS. Inclement weather and rough water conditions make a difference. More in-depth courses are offered by the Coast Guard Auxiliary, United States Power Squadrons, or your local State Boating Agency.

We strongly recommend that you have an experienced boater with you on your first few boat outings. Having an experienced boater on board will strengthen your confidence; allow you to gain valuable "hands-on" operation of your vessel; and will assist you in applying safe boating techniques and skills from the very first moment you set out on the water.

It makes no difference if you are the new skipper of a 16-foot outboard vessel, a 24-foot inboard vessel, or a 20-foot sailboat, safe boating is all the same - IT'S UP TO YOU!

*This text contains the most up-to-date information at the time of printing. In this constantly changing environment, some information may be modified. Be sure to check the most current regulations.

INTRODUCTION

Safe boating is an attitude of responsibility which is visible to others through your actions. It is an awareness of the consequences of your actions and the actions of others. As a safe boater you have a responsibility to your passengers: a responsibility to protect them from harm as the result of either your actions, their own actions, or the actions of others. Responsible safe boating is a matter of taking boating seriously, yet still enjoying the thrill, fun and excitement of the sport.

An objective of this course is for you to understand the fundamental principles of safe boating, and how to translate these principles into safe practices.

The "SKIPPER'S COURSE" is a self-paced instructional program. The subject material is divided into short sections. In each section you are asked to review specific amounts of information, and then answer the questions provided in the review exercises located at the end of each section. You will be able to check your responses immediately by looking in Appendix A. If you answered incorrectly, review and understand the material before continuing. You can work at your own pace and may stop at any time. There is an End of Course Examination to test your understanding of what is contained in this book.

DIRECTIONS:

- Review a section.

- Take the review exercise located at the end of the section.

- Check your answers in Appendix A.

- Review information for questions you may have answered incorrectly.

- Continue this process with each section.

- Proceed at your own pace.

- To receive your "SKIPPER'S COURSE" certificate, complete the End of Course Exam and mail to:

United States Coast Guard Auxiliary
9449 Watson Industrial Park
St. Louis, MO 63126

Boating Basics

CHAPTER 1

INTRODUCTION

Boating is more than just a sport; it's a form of transportation. Therefore, there are laws and requirements that apply. These laws and requirements were established to promote safe boating practices and protect the environment. To understand these regulations, a knowledge of boats, boat parts and systems as well as nautical terminology is essential. Some questions to consider are:

- What are the different boating terms?

- What is the difference between a planing and displacement hull, and why is this information important?

- What are the different categories of boats?

- How does one determine the capacity of a boat?

HULL: The main body of a vessel.

DRAFT: The depth of water a boat draws.

DISPLACEMENT HULL: A boat supported by its own buoyancy while in motion.

CATAMARAN: A twin-hulled boat, with hulls side by side.

DISPLACEMENT: The weight of water displaced by a floating hull.

PLANING HULL: A type of hull shaped to glide easily across the water at high speed.

KEEL: The centerline of a boat, running fore and aft; the backbone of a vessel.

The answers to these questions can be found in this chapter. Throughout this book there may be nautical terms with which you may not be familiar. You should learn these now so that you may fully understand this chapter and those to follow. They are common, everyday terms that are used in boating. Each has a specific meaning that will be understood by other boaters. You will find the definition of these terms in the margin on the page where they first appear. In addition, these terms are located in the "glossary" at the end of this book.

BOAT HULLS

Various boats handle differently, primarily because of their **hull** designs. There are two different types of boat hulls — displacement hulls and planing. Generally speaking, all boats and ships can be categorized by the way they are supported in the water when moving.

Displacement Hulls

Boats are supported by the water they displace. Some boats float higher in the water and do not have much **draft**. Others are designed to have more draft or displace more water. Boats that are designed to plow through the water are **displacement hulls**, and include rounded or V-shaped rowboats, sailboats, big ships, trawlers and some canoes, kayaks and **catamarans**.

Boats having a large **displacement** generally ride more comfortably without pounding, even in rough seas. Boats designed to operate strictly in the displacement mode can cross a wave or wake at a 45-degree angle and maintain control.

Planing Hulls

Boats designed to operate so that the pressure of the water against the bottom of the hull provides some support, are called **planing hulls**. When a planing hull is not moving, it is supported by the water it displaces (like a displacement hull). As it begins to move faster and faster, a larger percentage of its weight is supported by the pressure of the water against the bottom, much like a flat stone skipping along over the surface. A boat traveling in this manner is ON PLANE.

NOTE: Exercise caution while operating the boat during the transition from displacement to planing. Visibility will be temporarily limited as the bow rises out of the water.

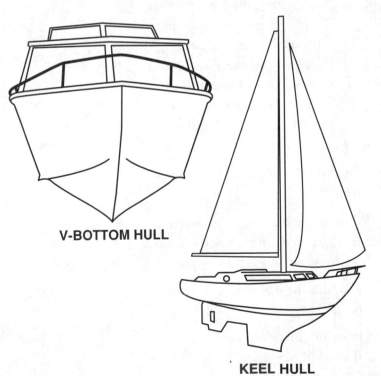

V-BOTTOM HULL

KEEL HULL

The three phases of a planing hull are:

1. Stopped or slow: displacement

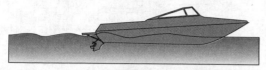

2. Transitional: **bow** is up, visibility is poor, **stern** digs in

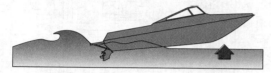

3. Plane: vessel is leveling, running smoothly

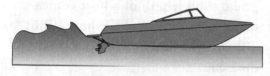

When slowing or stopping, the hull will settle quickly. Watch that the **wake** does not overtake and **swamp** the boat. To avoid swamping the boat, slow the speed of the boat gradually.

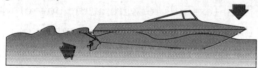

Planing hulls are specially designed hulls which tend to "ride up" on the water as they move through it faster and faster. A planing hull tends to "fly" over the surface, buoyed up by its own forward motion more than by the water it displaces. There are many types of planing hulls. Most are characterized by fairly extensive flat surfaces, although these may be angled to form a "V" shape in the water. A flat bottom will not handle well in difficult conditions, e.g. heavy wake. To maintain control of a flat bottom boat on plane while crossing a wave or wake, approach the wave at a

90-degree angle. To provide better handling, engineers have designed several hull variations:

There are a few boats, not shown here,

FLAT BOTTOM HULL

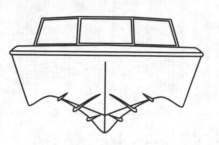

CATHEDRAL HULL

which travel fast enough so the effect of the air pressure against the hull provides support. The big racing hydroplane is a good example of this type.

Although displacement and planing are the two hull types, there are interesting variations. Some boats have two hulls and are called catamarans; others with three hulls are **trimarans**. Marine architects are always creating new combinations; however, operators should recognize that each design has its own handling characteristics. While many of these designs will allow boats to go faster and plane at lower speeds, they can also make them harder to handle in rough water. The placement of additional equipment and fuel tanks can also change the handling characteristics of various types of boats.

BOW: *The forward part of the boat.*

STERN: *The after part of the boat.*

WAKE: *Moving waves, track or path that a boat leaves behind it, when moving across the water.*

SWAMP: *To fill with water, but not settle to the bottom.*

TRIMARAN: *A boat with three hulls.*

CATAMARAN

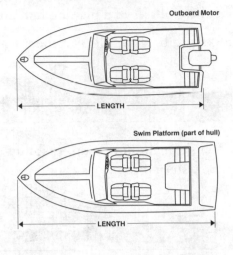

Outboard Motor

LENGTH

Swim Platform (part of hull)

LENGTH

REVIEW EXERCISE:

BOAT HULLS

1. Boats can be classified as _____ hulls or _____ hulls, depending on the way they ride in the water.

2. Boats that are designed to plow through the water are _____ hulls.

3. The three phases of a planing hull are:

    a. _____

    b. _____

    c. _____

BOAT CATEGORIES

The Coast Guard sets minimum safety standards for boats and associated equipment. To meet these standards some of the equipment must be Coast Guard approved.

Boat length often dictates required equipment. For equipment requirement purposes, motorboats are categorized in four size ranges:

Four Categories of Boats	
FEET	**METERS**
Less than 16 ft.	or 4.9 meters
16 ft. to less than 26 ft.	or 7.9 meters
26 ft. to less than 40 ft.	or 12.2 meters
40 ft. to no longer than 65 ft.	or 19.8 meters

Anything over 65 feet is no longer referred to as a "boat" or small craft.

Shown next are illustrations of an open, outboard motorboat and an inboard/outboard motorboat.

Notice that the outboard motor is NOT included in the measurement. The overall length of a boat is measured from the tip of the **bow** (front) in a straight line to the **stern** (back) of the boat.

The next illustration is an outline of an auxiliary sailboat (one with motor), to show examples of attachments NOT included in the overall length when determining the category of the boat. The **bowsprit** or anchor platform (extends forward at the bow of the boat to increase the potential for sail areas), and the attachment of the outboard motor on the stern is not included in the overall length.

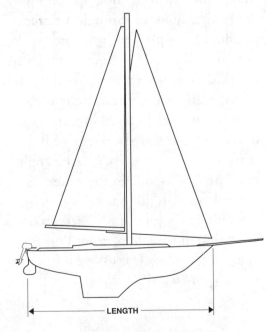

LENGTH

AUXILIARY SAILBOAT

CATEGORY OF BOATS

1. The prescribed equipment on board a boat is often determined by the _____ of the boat.

2. List the categories of boats by size:
   Less than _____ ft.
   _____ ft. to less than _____ ft.
   _____ ft. to less than _____ ft.
   _____ ft. to no longer than _____ ft.

3. Which measurement is correct in determining the length of a vessel: (circle one)

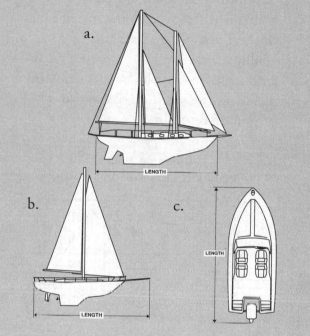

a.

b.

c.

CAPACITY PLATE

The number of seats in the boat is NOT a reliable indicator of how many people it can <u>safely</u> carry. There are two good ways to determine the number of people that may be safely accommodated in a boat under normal conditions. One is the boat manufacturer's capacity plate. **Monohull** boats less than 20 feet and built after November 1, 1972, except sailboats, canoes, kayaks and inflatables, will have a plate that looks like this:

This plate is mounted so that it is clearly visible to the operator. Notice the capacity plate states the recommended MAXIMUM number of people or pounds that the boat can safely carry, under normal conditions.

The capacity plate makes several assumptions:

• The engine is no larger than the maximum horsepower (hp) listed.

NOTE: Maximum horsepower will appear only on capacity plates of outboard boats.

• There is a normal amount of fuel, equipment and supplies on board.

• Wind, water and weather conditions are nearly perfect.

• The APPROXIMATE weight of people in the boat is 150 pounds each.

There are a lot of assumptions. These assumptions mean that you, the skipper, must exercise careful judgement when deciding the number of passengers that may be safely transported. The skipper is always responsible for the passengers' safety.

BOWSPRIT: A spar extending forward from the bow.

MONOHULL: A boat with one hull.

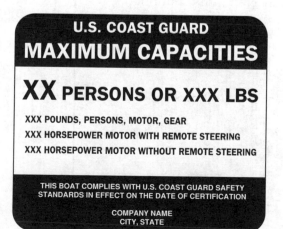

U.S. COAST GUARD

MAXIMUM CAPACITIES

XX PERSONS OR XXX LBS

XXX POUNDS, PERSONS, MOTOR, GEAR
XXX HORSEPOWER MOTOR WITH REMOTE STEERING
XXX HORSEPOWER MOTOR WITHOUT REMOTE STEERING

THIS BOAT COMPLIES WITH U.S. COAST GUARD SAFETY STANDARDS IN EFFECT ON THE DATE OF CERTIFICATION

COMPANY NAME
CITY, STATE

BEAM: The greatest width of the boat.

TRANSOM: The stern cross-section of a square-sterned boat.

NOTE: In severe conditions, even the number on the capacity plate may be unsafe. If the weather is severe, it may not be safe to take the boat out at all!!

If there is no capacity plate, and you wish to estimate the maximum number of people the boat can safely carry, multiply the **length** by the **width** or **beam**, then divide by 15.

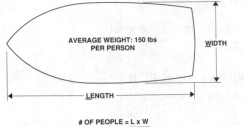

AVERAGE WEIGHT: 150 lbs PER PERSON
WIDTH
LENGTH

OF PEOPLE = $\frac{L \times W}{15}$

Number of people in boat

After making the calculations, write the number on white tape and stick it near the operator's position as a reminder for safe loading.

There will be more about properly loading a boat in Chapter 5.

REMEMBER: Both the capacity plate and this formula are based on ideal weather conditions.

HULL IDENTIFICATION NUMBER (HIN)

The HIN is a 12-character number that identifies the boat's hull. It is not to be confused with the state registration number displayed on the bow of the boat. On boats with a **transom**, the primary HIN must be permanently affixed to the top right side within two inches of the top of the transom. The secondary HIN is permanently affixed to the interior of the hull in a place where it is not readily noticeable. The number assists authorities in case the boat is damaged or stolen. Record the HIN for your boat and keep it in a safe place.

Common HIN:
stamped into fiberglass of transom

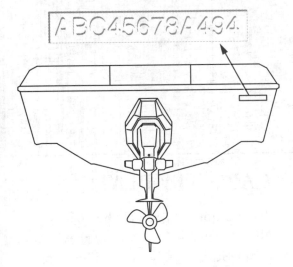

ABC45678A494

REVIEW EXERCISE:
CAPACITY PLATE

1. The two ways to determine a boat's capacity are:

   a. _____

   b. _____

2. Capacity plates state the recommended _____ number of people or _____ that a boat can safely carry, under normal conditions.

3. A 20 foot boat with a 6 foot beam can safely carry:

   a. 7 people   c. 9 people

   b. 8 people   d. 10 people

SUMMARY

BOATING BASICS

This chapter covered some boating basics. It stated that in order to understand the laws and regulations which apply to boating, a basic knowledge of boats and boat parts, and an understanding of nautical terms is needed.

Two types of boat hulls covered included:

Displacement - plows through the water.

Planing - pressure of water against hull provides some support.

The three stages of the planing hull include stopped or slow, transitional, and plane.

The four categories of recreational boats range from less than 16 feet (4.9 meters) to 65 feet (19.8 meters). Anything over 65 feet is no longer referred to as a "boat" or small craft.

The number of persons a boat can safely carry is determined either by using the formula:

$$\# \text{ of people} = \frac{\text{Length x Width}}{15}$$

or reading the manufacturer's capacity plate. The capacity plate assumes there are ideal weather conditions. The number of seats in the boat is NOT a reliable indicator of how many people the boat can safely carry.

It can't be overemphasized that it is the skipper that is always responsible for the passenger's safety.

With these basic principles in mind, we are now ready to cover such topics as Legal Requirements, Water Activities, Weather, and Trailering Your Boat, to name a few.

Legal Requirements

CHAPTER 2

INTRODUCTION

The Federal Government, states, and many local communities have laws and regulations designed to keep recreational boating a safe sport. In addition to the requirements stated in this chapter, the owner and operator may be required to comply with additional regulations specific to the state in which the vessel is registered or operated. This chapter also provides the information needed for a minimum amount of personal protection; however, these minimum standards offer no guarantee of a boater's survival on the waterway. Remember, requirements may vary from state to state. To insure compliance with state boating laws, contact the appropriate boating agency (See Appendix E).

PERSONAL FLOTATION DEVICE (PFD): Official terminology for life jacket. When properly used, will support a person in the water. Available in several sizes and types.

FLAME ARRESTER: A safety device, such as a metal mesh protector to prevent an exhaust backfire from causing an explosion; operates by absorbing heat.

Requirements for boats are very similar to those for automobiles. When a driver puts a car on the road, it is his responsibility to make sure it is properly registered, has license plates, and meets required safety standards. In a similar fashion, boats must also be registered or documented. However, the safety equipment needed on board may vary depending on the length of the boat and on its power source.

Federal and state laws require the boat be equipped with:

- Basic safety devices, e.g.. **Personal Flotation Devices** (PFDs), fire extinguishers, etc.

NOTE: For additional information refer to, U.S. Coast Guard publication, "Federal Requirements and Safety Tips for Recreational Boats."

- Proper ventilation systems and backfire **flame arresters**, and

- Navigation lights

The Coast Guard Auxiliary offers the Courtesy Marine Examination (CME), to help you comply with the above. For additional information, contact your local Coast Guard Auxiliary or call the U.S. Coast Guard Boating Safety Infoline (1-800-368-5647).

NUMBERING

By Federal law, recreational vessels 5 net tons or over may be documented with the Coast Guard. All other boats equipped with a motor must be numbered in the state of principal use. (NOTE: In some states all boats must be registered.) Boats are numbered so they can be identified. Boats are registered and numbered in much

the same manner that a car is registered. Proper forms can be obtained from state boating authorities (Appendix E). Upon completion of standard forms accompanied with the appropriate fee, a Certificate of Number is issued.

These numbers and letters must be painted or permanently attached to the forward half of the boat, so that they read left to right. They must be in block characters, in a color that contrasts with the boat hull background color and no smaller than 3 inches high. Be sure to leave a space, or hyphen, between the first set of letters and the numbers that follow, as well as between the numbers and the last set of letters. The space (width) should be about the size of the letter "M." Paint or mount the registration number on each side of the bow similar to the examples below.

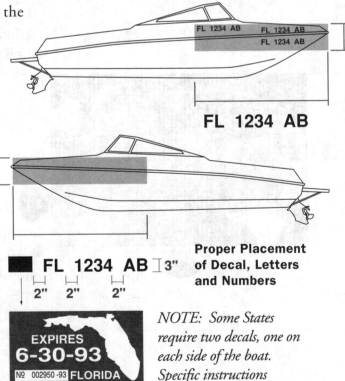

Recommended Locations for Registration Numbers

FL 1234 AB

Proper Placement of Decal, Letters and Numbers

NOTE: Some States require two decals, one on each side of the boat. Specific instructions pertaining to decal placement in your state can often be found on the adhesive backing of the registration decal.

Number placement on bow

Don't use fancy lettering. It is too hard to read and will not be accepted by the Coast Guard or state boating officials.

In addition, a state may issue an annual registration sticker to be placed with the registration numbers.

The state will also issue a paper Certificate of Number. This certificate must be on board the boat while it is in use. This certificate is normally the first document a marine law enforcement officer will ask to see if you are stopped or boarded.

When selling or transferring a boat, The Certificate of Number must be returned to the state. Another Certificate of Number will be issued to the new owner.

REVIEW EXERCISE: NUMBERING

1. Print this imaginary boat number in the proper manner on the bow shown below.

CA8934AC

2. What is the first thing a Marine Law Enforcement Officer will normally ask to see when stopping and boarding a boat?

_____

3. The numbers and letters are required to be:
   a. _____
   b. _____
   c. _____
   d. _____
   e. _____
   f. _____

REQUIRED EQUIPMENT

A boat must contain the proper equipment so that it can be legally operated on the water. The law requires certain minimum equipment in the boat. The equipment required depends on the length of the boat and its power source. The required equipment will be discussed individually in the following paragraphs.

Personal Flotation Devices (PFDs)

Anyone who has ever fallen out of a boat, or been in a boat that **capsized**, knows the value of wearing a Personal Flotation Device (PFD) or life jacket. Each person on board must have a PFD. Although not required to be worn, A PROPERLY FITTED PFD SHOULD BE WORN AT ALL TIMES WHEN THE VESSEL IS **UNDERWAY**. Certain Type V PFDs (Hybrid) are required to be worn at all times when underway. A wearable PFD can save a life, but only if it is on and fits properly.

PFDs must be Coast Guard approved, in good and serviceable condition, and the appropriate size for the intended

CAPSIZE: To turn over.

UNDERWAY: Vessel in motion, i.e., when not moored, at anchor, or aground.

STOW: To pack or store away; especially, to pack in an orderly, compact manner.

GEAR: A general term for ropes, blocks, tackle and other equipment.

user. Wearable PFDs must be readily accessible, which means that in an emergency (boat sinking, fire, etc.), the passengers must be able to reach them easily and quickly. PFDs should not be **stowed** in plastic bags, in locked or closed compartments or have other **gear** stowed on top of them. To be of any value, a PFD must be worn. Statistics show that over eighty-five percent (85%) of people involved in fatal boating accidents were not wearing PFDs.

Throwable devices must be immediately available for use under federal and many state laws.

Let's look at the different types of PFDs.

Type I

A Type I PFD, or OFF-SHORE LIFE JACKET, provides the most buoyancy (capacity to float). It is effective for all waters, especially open, rough or remote waters where rescue may be delayed. Under normal conditions, it is designed to turn and to support most unconscious wearers in the water to a face-up position. Both adult and child sizes are available. The adult size provides at least 22 pounds buoyancy, the child size, 11 pounds, minimum.

Type II

A Type II PFD, or NEAR-SHORE BUOYANT VEST, is intended for calm water, or where there is a good chance of quick rescue. This type will turn SOME unconscious wearers, in some circumstances, to a face-up position in the water. The turning action is not as pronounced, nor will it turn as many persons to a face-up position as a Type I would under the same conditions. An adult size device provides at least 15 pounds buoyancy, a medium child size provides 11

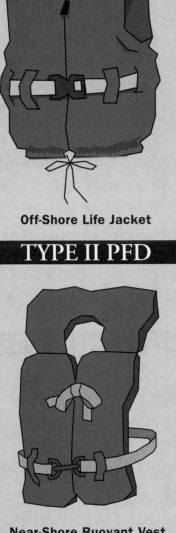

TYPE I PFD

Off-Shore Life Jacket

TYPE II PFD

Near-Shore Buoyant Vest

TYPE III PFD

Flotation Aid

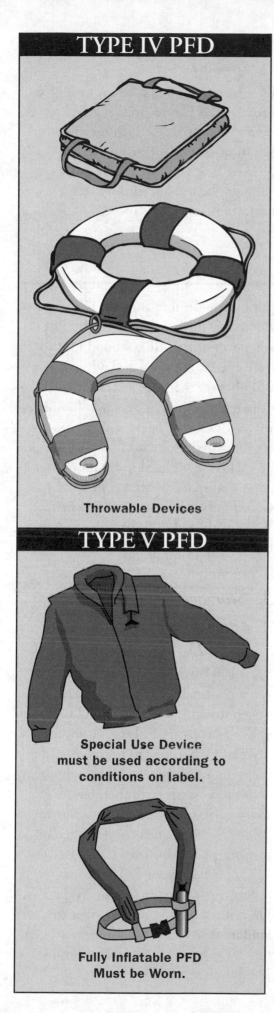

TYPE IV PFD

Throwable Devices

TYPE V PFD

Special Use Device must be used according to conditions on label.

Fully Inflatable PFD Must be Worn.

pounds. Infant and small child sizes each provide at least 7 pounds buoyancy.

Type III

A Type III, or FLOTATION AID, is good for calm, inland water, or where there is a good chance of quick rescue. They are designed so wearers can easily place themselves in a face-up position in the water. The wearer may have to tilt their head back to avoid turning face-down in the water. The Type III has the same minimum buoyancy as a Type II PFD. It comes in many styles, colors and sizes and is generally the most comfortable type for continuous wear. Type IIIs are often designed for specific sports, such as hunting, fishing, waterskiing, and canoeing. Different vest and float coat styles are available.

Type IV

A Type IV PFD, or THROWABLE DEVICE, is intended for calm, inland water with heavy boat traffic, where help is always present. It is designed to be thrown to a person in the water who can grasp and hold it until rescued. Even though Type IVs can be grasped for support, they are not designed to be worn. Type IV devices include buoyant cushions, ring buoys and horseshoe buoys.

Practice throwing the Type IV PFD. It should be thrown underhand. (Keep in mind that all types of PFDs can be thrown, and throwing all types should be practiced.)

Type V

A Type V PFD, or SPECIAL USE DEVICE is intended for specific activities and may be carried instead of another PFD <u>only if used according to the approval conditions on the label.</u>

HYPOTHERMIA: A life-threatening condition in which the body's warming mechanisms fail to maintain normal body temperature and the entire body cools.

2•5

DECK: A permanent covering over a compartment, hull or any part of a boat serving as a floor.

ABOARD: On or within the boat.

Some Type V devices provide significant **hypothermia** protection. Varieties include **deck** suits, work vests, board sailing vests, and Hybrid PFDs.

A Type V HYBRID INFLATABLE PFD is the least bulky of all PFD types. It contains a small amount of inherent buoyancy and an inflatable chamber. Its performance is equal to a Type I, II, or III PFD (as noted on the PFD label) when inflated. Hybrid PFDs must be worn when underway to be acceptable.

Other Type V PFDs are approved for activities and conditions marked on them. Examples of this type are flotation coveralls (for warmth), boardsailing vests and rafting vests. All must be used according to the limitations on their labels.

What A Smart Skipper Knows About PFDs

1. How many PFDs are needed?

Boats less than 16 feet in length (including canoes and kayaks of any length) are required to carry wearable PFDs for each person on board.

Otherwise, if a boat is 16 feet and longer, it must be equipped with one Type I, II, III, or V PFD for each person aboard — PLUS one Type IV device. It is recommended that each person be fitted with a wearable device.

2. Who should wear a PFD?

Everyone should wear a PFD — especially children and non-swimmers of all ages. On small boats this is particularly important. All non-swimmers should wear PFDs at all times when in a boat. Passengers who are physically disabled may have special flotation needs. They should have PFDs which they have tried in a swimming pool prior to going on board. If they are unable to quickly put on the devices alone or while in the water, they should wear the PFDs whenever afloat. It is a good idea to have everyone try on and adjust their PFD before the boat leaves the dock or launch area. PFDs should be worn with all straps, zippers and ties fastened. The loose ends of straps should be tucked in. The skipper should set a good example and wear a PFD. Coast Guard personnel wear PFDs whenever they are **aboard** a Coast Guard vessel measuring 65 feet (19.8 meters) or less.

3. Stowage and Care of PFDs

Most PFDs will last a long time if given reasonable care. Let PFDs drip dry thoroughly before putting them away. Make sure PFDs are stowed in a dry place when not in use. Never dry them on a radiator, heater or any other direct heat source. Stow them in a well-ventilated place. Before stowing PFDs, check for tears and broken or torn straps. Dispose of damaged PFDs. Never use a PFD as a cushion, unless it is meant to be one (Type IV). Do not use a PFD as a bumper or **fender** since the flotation material can be crushed, causing loss of buoyancy. Do not alter a PFD.

FENDER: A cushion, placed between boats, or between a boat and a pier, to prevent damage.

GALLEY: The kitchen area of a boat.

Sound Devices

There will be times, because of limited visibility (such as fog, mist or heavy rain), when boaters are required to make loud sound signals to warn other boaters of their locations.

A boat less than 39.4 feet (12 meters) must have some means of making an efficient sound signal. A whistle will do; a bell is not required.

A boat 40 feet to less than 66 feet (20 meters) must have a powered whistle or horn which is audible for 0.5 nautical miles. A bell is also required. Horns can be of the canister or electric-powered variety.

In general, sound-producing devices are not Coast Guard approved and don't have Coast Guard approval numbers. The only criterion is that boats have a device aboard which meets the legal requirements for their size category. Even if not required by law, some type of sound device should be on board.

Fire Extinguishers

The danger of fire on board a boat is much greater than in a car. Fuel vapors can collect in the bilge of the boat because these vapors are heavier than air. For this reason, Coast Guard-approved fire extinguishers are required on all motorboats where explosive or flammable gases or vapors can be trapped. They're also protection against electrical or **galley** fires.

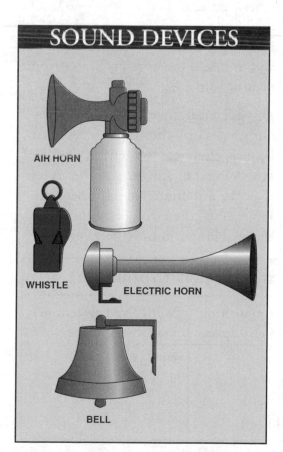

SOUND DEVICES

AIR HORN

WHISTLE

ELECTRIC HORN

BELL

THWART: A seat or brace running laterally across a boat.

SECURE: To make fast.

Approved extinguishers are classified by letter and number symbols. The letter indicates the type of fire the unit is designed to extinguish. (Type B, for example, is designed to extinguish flammable liquids, such as gasoline, oil and grease fires.) The number indicates the relative size of the extinguisher (minimum extinguishing agent weight).

TYPE A — Fires of ordinary combustible materials such as wood or paper

TYPE B — Gasoline, oil and grease fires

TYPE C — Electrical fires

Coast Guard-approved extinguishers are portable, either B-I or B-II classification, and have a specific marine type mounting bracket. All extinguishers should be mounted in a readily accessible location.

U.S.C.G.-Approved Extinguishers

Classes	Foam (gals)	CO2 (lbs)	Dry Chemical (lbs)
B-I	1.75	4	2
B-II	2.5	15	10

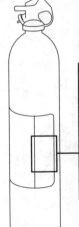

MARINE TYPE USCG
TYPE B:C   SIZE I
APPROVAL NO. 162.028/
EX2397. VALID ONLY
WITH BRACKETS BTO2O,
BTO22, OR BTO24.

(UL) UNDERWRITERS LABORATORIES INC.®
LISTED

1990

Coast Guard-approved extinguishers are identified by the following markings on the label:

NOTE: Underwriters Laboratory — 'UL Listed' does not necessarily mean Coast Guard approved.

Fire extinguishers must be carried on ALL motorboats that meet one or more of the following conditions:

- An inboard engine
- Closed compartments under **thwarts** and seats where portable fuel tanks may be stored
- Double bottoms not sealed to the hull or which are not completely filled with flotation materials
- Closed living spaces
- Closed stowage compartments in which combustible or flammable materials are stored
- Permanently installed fuel tanks

*NOTE: Fuel tanks **secured** so they cannot be moved in case of fire or other emergency are considered permanently installed. There is no gallon capacity limit to determine if a fuel tank is portable. If the weight of a fuel tank is such that persons on board cannot move it, the Coast Guard considers it permanently installed.*

Check extinguishers regularly to insure the needle indicators on the gauges are in the "pie-shaped" operating range and to insure the nozzles are free from obstructions.

Dry-chemical fire extinguishers without gauges or indicating devices must be inspected every 6 months. If the gross weight of any extinguisher is less than the minimum amount specified on its label, the extinguisher is not acceptable and must be recharged.

Federal Requirements for Fire Extinguishers (Minimum)

Class	Length of Vessel	No fixed fire extinguishing system in machinery space	With fixed system in machinery space
A	Less than 16ft.	1 B-I	none
1	16ft. to under 26ft.	1 B-I	none
2	26ft. to under 40ft.	2 B-I or 1 B-II	1 B-I
3	40ft. to 65 ft.	3 B-I or 1 B-I and 1 B-II	2 B-I or 1 B-II

CHARGE INDICATORS

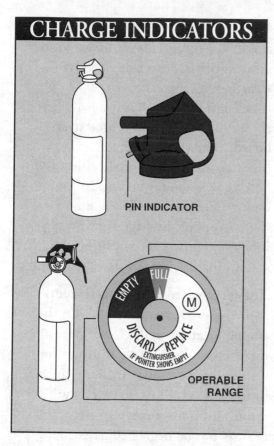

PIN INDICATOR

OPERABLE RANGE

NOTE: Weigh extinguishers annually to assure that the minimum weight is as stated on the extinguisher label.

Positioning Fire Extinguishers

Locate fire extinguishers where they are easily accessible. Be sure to place them away from potential sources of fire *(see diagram on page 2-10).*

Make frequent checks to be sure they are in their proper mounting brackets and undamaged. Cracked or broken hoses should be replaced. Locking pins and sealing wires should be checked to make sure that the extinguisher has not been used since last recharged.

Extinguishers should never be tested just to see if they are in proper operating condition. The valve might not reset, which would result in a slow leak. A discharged extinguisher must be recharged right away!

REVIEW EXERCISE:

FIRE EXTINGUISHERS

Identify the number and type of fire extinguishers required for the illustrations below.

1. This is an illustration of a 24-foot open cruiser with an inboard gasoline engine and permanent fuel tank installed. It does not have a fixed fire extinguishing system installed.

   Type _____
   Number_____

   Type _____ Number_____

2. Shown here is an open outboard runabout 14 feet in length with a closed fuel compartment.

   Type _____
   Number_____

   Type _____ Number_____

3. Shown here is an illustration of a 50-foot cabin cruiser with a fixed fire extinguishing system installed in the machinery spaces.

   Type _____
   Number _____

   Type _____ Number_____

4. Shown here is an illustration of a 35- foot auxiliary sailboat. It is powered by sails and a small inboard engine without a fixed fire extinguishing system in the engine space.

   Type _____
   Number_____

   Type _____ Number_____

5. Extinguishers should be tested just to see if they are in proper operating condition. ☐ True ☐ False

BILGE: The interior of the hull below the floor boards.

COWL: An air scoop designed to improve ventilation intake and exhaust vents.

OVERBOARD: Over the side or out of the boat.

OUTDRIVE: A propulsion system for boats, with an inboard engine operating an exterior drive, with driveshaft, gears, and propeller; also called stern-drive and inboard/ outboard.

DOCK: A protected water area in which vessels are moored. The term is often used to denote a pier or a wharf.

Ventilation

The greatest cause of fire and explosions aboard recreational boats is gasoline vapor collecting in the lower compartments of the boat (**bilges**).

Gasoline vapor is heavier than air and sinks to the lower compartments. If a flow of air isn't present to blow gas vapor out of the boat, then the vapor sits there waiting for a spark — which could come from sources such as a cigarette ash or an electric switch. Vapor will collect in the bilge if compartments are not properly ventilated.

No completely foolproof ventilation system has yet been developed. However, ventilation systems are required by law because they <u>do</u> reduce the chance of explosion <u>significantly</u>.

Fresh air is directed into engine and fuel tank compartments using wind scoops (**cowls**), often assisted by electric blowers to move the air. A tube leads to the exhaust cowl where the collected vapor is vented **overboard**. The tubes connecting the lower areas with the intake and exhaust cowls should be at least two inches in diameter. The diagram at the bottom of the page shows a typical inboard engine with a ventilation system that includes a fixed fuel tank.

The same ventilation requirements apply to auxiliary sailboats, but, the engine location in the lower part of the deep hull can make routing the ventilation ducts very difficult as seen in the sailboat illustration below. It is important that ventilation in this type of boat not be neglected. Because

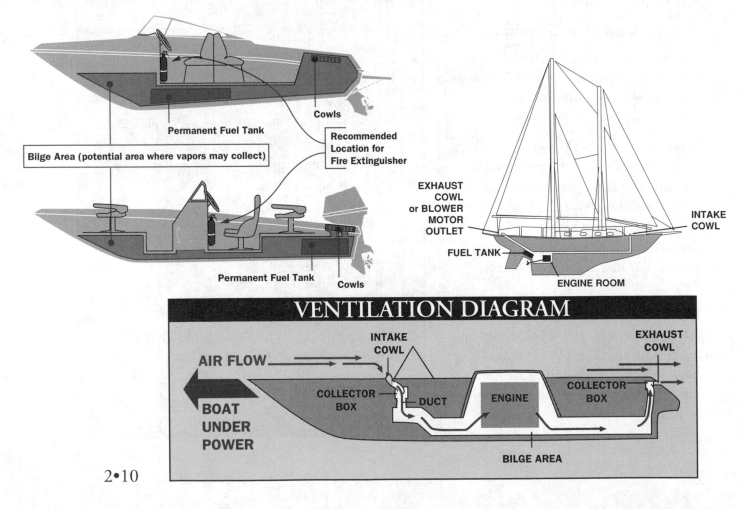

Permanent Fuel Tank

Cowls

Bilge Area (potential area where vapors may collect)

Recommended Location for Fire Extinguisher

Permanent Fuel Tank

Cowls

EXHAUST COWL or BLOWER MOTOR OUTLET

INTAKE COWL

FUEL TANK

ENGINE ROOM

VENTILATION DIAGRAM

INTAKE COWL

EXHAUST COWL

AIR FLOW

BOAT UNDER POWER

COLLECTOR BOX

DUCT

ENGINE

COLLECTOR BOX

BILGE AREA

2•10

sailboats spend a great deal of time operating with the engine shut down, air circulation, created by the engine "breathing" is nonexistent. When the wind dies and the engine must be started, it is critical that the motor compartment is free of vapors. Adequate ventilation is of primary importance in sailboats with auxiliary (engine) power as well as in powerboats.

Special vapor and explosion-proof electric fans are required with inboard and inboard-outboard engines. Remember: when choosing a powered blower, be sure it has a marine-type, spark-proof switch.

A ventilation system will not remove spilled fuel or oil from the bilge or bottom of a boat!! WIPE UP ANY SPILLED FUEL OR OIL! On larger vessels with a galley, make sure that storage compartments containing cooking fuels are well ventilated.

REMEMBER:

(1) Always ventilate the engine compartment before turning on any switches or starting the engine;

(2) Operate the bilge blower for at least four minutes before starting an inboard engine;

(3) "Sniff" your bilges. Usually your nose is the best fuel and vapor detector.

REVIEW EXERCISE:

VENTILATION

1. Fuel is most dangerous when it turns into a _____.

2. The best way to prevent danger from fuel vapor is to have adequate _____.

3. Fuel in boats is always a safety hazard because the vapor is _____ than air and can collect in lower compartments where any spark can cause_____.

4. A powered blower for ventilation should have a_____ switch.

Backfire Flame Control

If a boat has a gasoline INBOARD or INBOARD-OUTBOARD engine, it must be equipped with an acceptable means of backfire flame control, which usually means that a Coast Guard-approved flame arrester should be on the carburetor. An OUTBOARD or diesel engine, does not require a flame arrester.

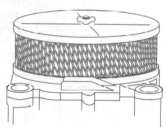

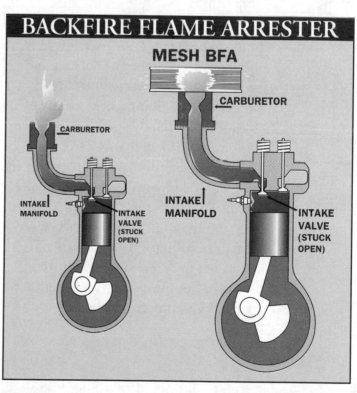

BACKFIRE FLAME ARRESTER

MESH BFA

CARBURETOR

CARBURETOR

INTAKE MANIFOLD

INTAKE VALVE (STUCK OPEN)

INTAKE MANIFOLD

INTAKE VALVE (STUCK OPEN)

WARNING: Every effort should be made to eliminate possible ignition sources of flammable vapors and materials on board the boat. For this reason, only <u>marine-rated</u> engine parts should be used. <u>Marine-rated</u> parts such as alternators and starters are shielded to prevent sparking.

NOTE: Not only are flame arresters approved, but carburetors, alternators and starters should also be rated for Marine service. All electrical equipment should be ignition proof.

Visual Distress Signals (VDS)

Visual Distress Signals allow boaters to signal for help during an emergency. Visual Distress Signals (VDS) can be seen during the day or night and are additional safeguards for the boater.

VDS may be pyrotechnic (combustible — such as smoke or flame), and nonpyrotechnic (noncombustible — such as a flag).

This section describes the rules for VDS, and includes the specific use of each type.

U.S.C.G.-approved VDS are required on all vessels used on coastal waters, the Great Lakes, territorial seas and those waters connected directly to them up to a point where a body of water is less than 2 miles wide. Recreational boats less than 16 feet in length, open sailboats less than 26 feet not equipped with motors, manually propelled boats, and boats participating in organized events such as races, regattas, or marine parades are not required to carry day visual distress signals, but must carry night signals when operating from sunset to sunrise.

Pyrotechnic Visual Distress Signalling Devices

Pyrotechnic VDS devices must be U.S. Coast Guard-approved, maintained in serviceable condition, and stowed to be readily accessible. The date of the serviceable life must not have expired. Launchers which were produced prior to January 1, 1981 for use with approved signals need not be labeled as U.S. Coast Guard-approved.

U.S. Coast Guard-approved pyrotechnic visual distress signals and associated devices include:

- Pyrotechnic red **flares** (hand held or aerial)

- Pyrotechnic orange smoke (hand held or floating)

- Launchers for aerial red meteors or parachute flares

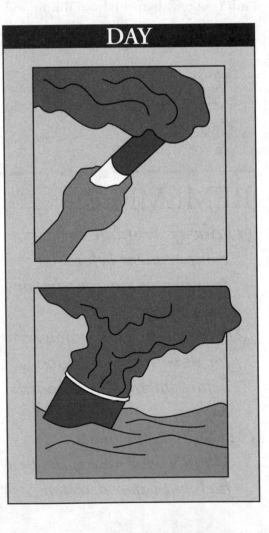

DAY

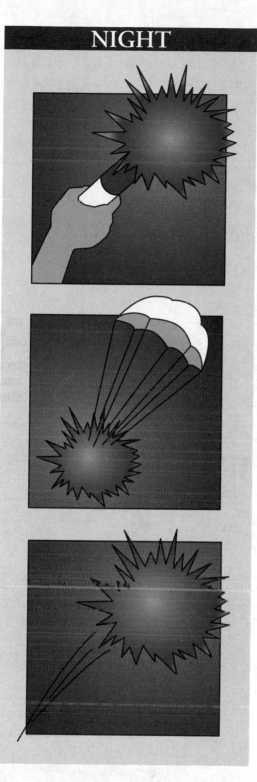

Red hand-held flares can be used by day but are most effective at night or in restricted visibility, such as fog or haze. When selecting flares, look for the Coast Guard Approval number, manufacturing and expiration dates.

Visual distress signals are not toys! Keep small children away from them! Never use them unless there is a genuine need for help.

Projected devices, such as pistol-launched and hand-held parachute flares and meteors, have many of the characteristics of a firearm and must be handled with the same caution and respect. In some states the pistol launcher for meteors and parachute flares may be considered a firearm. Therefore, check with state boating authorities before obtaining such a device.

Also, hand-held pyrotechnics may expel ash and slag as they burn. Even though these particles cool quickly, they can cause painful burns or ignite materials on the boat. The flare itself could start a fire if dropped. These devices should be held over the **LEEWARD** side in such a way that hot slag will not drip on the boater or the boat.

If pyrotechnic devices are selected, a minimum of three must be carried. Any combination can be carried as long as they add up to three signals for day, and three signals for night use. Three combination day/night signalling devices meet both requirements. If a VDS is necessary, use it wisely and follow the directions provided by the manufacturer for safe and effective use.

NOTE: Pyrotechnic devices do not burn very long.

The following examples illustrate the variety and combination of devices which can be carried in order to meet the requirements:

- Three hand-held flares (day and night)

- One hand-held red flare and two parachute flares (day and night)

- One hand-held orange smoke signal, two floating orange smoke signals (day) and one electric distress light (night only)

BOAT HOOK: A short shaft with a fitting at one end shaped to facilitate use in putting a line over a piling, recovering an object dropped overboard, or in pushing or fending off.

MAST: A spar set upright to support rigging and sails.

Non-Pyrotechnic Visual Distress Signalling Devices

Non-pyrotechnic visual distress signalling devices must carry a manufacturer's certification that they meet Coast Guard requirements. They must be in serviceable condition and be readily available for use.

1. Orange Distress Flag

The distress flag must be at least 3 x 3 feet with a black square and ball on an orange background. It is accepted as a day signal only and is especially effective in bright sunlight. The flag is most distinctive when hoisted on a paddle, **boat hook**, or flown from a **mast**.

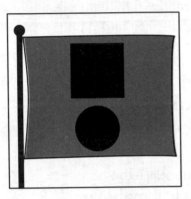

2. Electric Distress Light

The electric distress light is accepted for night use only and must automatically flash the international SOS distress signal, which is three short flashes, three long flashes, and three short flashes (• • • — — — • • •). Flashed four to six times each minute, this unmistakable distress signal is well known to most boaters and non-boaters alike. If shielded from view, this device can be checked any time for serviceability. An ordinary flashlight is not acceptable since it must be manually flashed and does not normally produce a bright enough light.

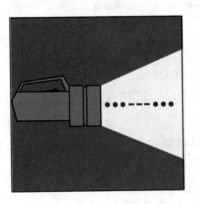

3. Other Visual Distress Signals

In addition to those signals which are specifically required and approved by the Coast Guard, there are a number of other signals that have been traditionally used which are also effective. However, these signals cannot replace those prescribed by regulation. They are:

- signal mirror
- arm waving
- code flags

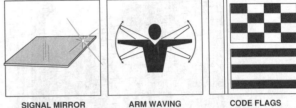

SIGNAL MIRROR   ARM WAVING   CODE FLAGS (NOVEMBER-CHARLIE)

REVIEW EXERCISE:
VISUAL DISTRESS SIGNALS

1. Day visual distress signals (VDS) are required on:

   a. vessels used on_____, _____, _____.

   b. an open sailboat equipped with an _____.

   c. recreational boats more than _____ feet in length.

2. If choosing pyrotechnic devices for compliance, a minimum of _____are required on board.

3. The international SOS distress signal is _____.

4. Hand-held pyrotechnics may expel ash and slag as they burn. These devices should be held in such a way that _____ _____.

Navigation Lights and Shapes

Navigation lights are required between sunset and sunrise, and during other periods of reduced visibility, such as fog, rain, haze, etc. The different lighting requirements are found in the U.S. Coast Guard Navigation Rules, International-Inland (COMDTINST M16672.2C).

Federal and state laws require that ALL boats display certain lights at night. These lights indicate the presence of a boat, the type of boat (sailboat, motorboat or rowboat), and the size of a boat. These lights, as seen on another boat, signal crossing, meeting, or overtaking.

Only four colors are used: red, green, white and yellow. The lights are designed so they only show in certain directions.

The SIDELIGHTS are red on the **port** (left) side and green on the **starboard** (right) side, each showing an unbroken light over an arc of 112.5 degrees from straight **ahead** to 22.5 degrees **abaft** of the beam on its respective side. The total arc of visibility for both sidelights is 225 degrees.

The STERNLIGHT is a white light placed as near as possible at the stern of the boat, showing an unbroken

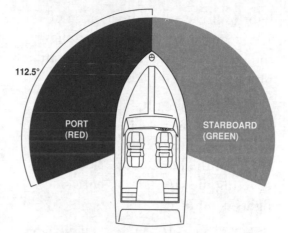

SIDE LIGHTS

PORT: The left side of a boat looking forward. A harbor.

STARBOARD: The right side of a boat when looking forward.

AHEAD: In a forward direction.

ABAFT: Behind. Toward the rear (stern) of the boat.

AFT: Toward the stern of the boat.

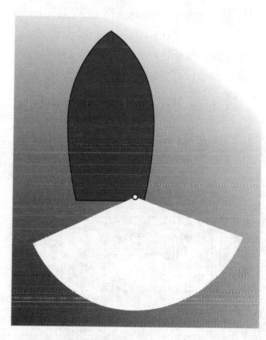

STERNLIGHT

65.6 Feet = 20 Meters

39.4 Feet = 12 Meters

VESSELS LESS THAN 65.6 FEET

LIGHT	VISIBLE RANGE in miles		ARC in degrees
	LESS THAN 39.4 Ft	39.4 Ft OR MORE	
Masthead Light	2	3	225
All-round Light	2	2	360
Sidelights	1	2	112.5
Sternlight	2	2	135

light over the arc of the horizon of 135 degrees, and so fixed as to show the light 67.5 degrees from right **aft** on each side of the vessel.

A MASTHEAD LIGHT is a white light placed over the **fore and aft** centerline of the vessel. It shows over an arc of the horizon of 225 degrees covering the same area as both side-lights combined.

A TOWING LIGHT is a yellow light and shows over the same arc as the sternlight and is placed above it (figure 1). There are also towing situations where two yellow lights, and no stern light, are displayed. When two yellow lights appear, a boat is being towed. STAY CLEAR!!

FIGURE 1

Lights that show over the full 360 degrees are ALL-ROUND LIGHTS. They can be any of the colors mentioned above depending on what the boat is doing.

For most recreational boats under 39.4 feet, the sidelights must be visible for one mile; all other lights must be visible for two miles.

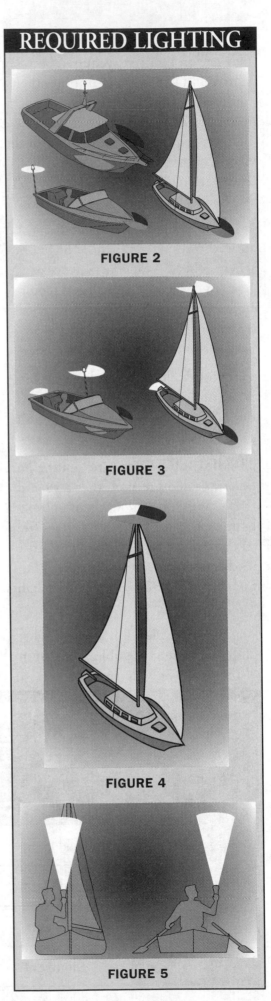

REQUIRED LIGHTING

FIGURE 2

FIGURE 3

FIGURE 4

FIGURE 5

Lights that boats must have installed to operate on inland waters are:

1. Power Boats or Sailboats running with a motor only, or under sail and motor

    a. If the boat is 39.4 feet or more in length, it shall exhibit lights as shown in Figure 3.

    b. Boats less than 39.4 feet, may show the lights in either Figure 2 or Figure 3.

2. Sailboats and Boats Under Manual Propulsion

    a. A sailboat less than 65.6 feet in length should show the navigation lights as in Figure 3 without the masthead light. The lights may be combined in a single lantern carried atop the mast as in Figure 4.

    b. A sailboat less than 23 feet in length, and a boat under manual propulsion should, if practical, show those lights described above. If not, an electric torch or lighted lantern, showing a white light, must be displayed in sufficient time to prevent collision, as in Figure 5.

FIGURE 6

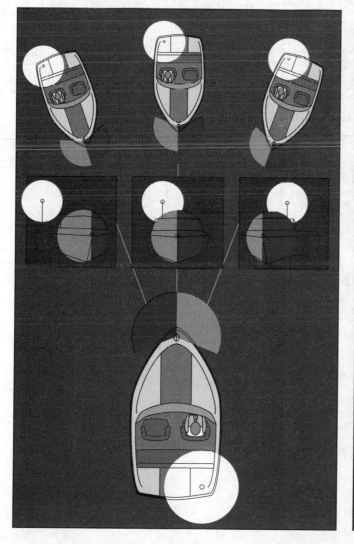

FIGURE 7

LIGHTS

1. Navigation lights are required between _____ and _____, and during periods of _____.

2. The four colors used for navigation lights are:
   1. _____
   2. _____
   3. _____
   4. _____

3. The four different arcs of visibility for navigation lights are:
   1. _____
   2. _____
   3. _____
   4. _____

4. When following DIRECTLY behind another boat at night, what color lights should be visible?_____

5. Look at this combination of lights. Which way is the boat traveling? *(circle one)*

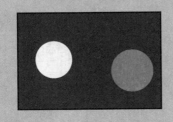

   a. _____ 👉

   b. 👈 _____

STATE REQUIREMENTS

As an owner of a recreational boat, it is necessary to comply with certain regulations specific to the state where the boat is registered or used. These regulations vary from state to state, depending on existing local conditions. To insure compliance with these various state laws, contact the State Boating Law Administrator (APPENDIX E) or local Coast Guard Auxiliary unit (Appendix C) to avoid any future problems.

RECOMMENDED EQUIPMENT

Besides meeting the minimum legal requirements, prudent boaters should carry some additional safety equipment, such as:

- **Portable Fuel Tanks.** These tanks should be constructed of durable material in sound condition. Any vents must be capable of being closed, and the tank must have a vapor-tight leakproof cap. Make sure the tanks are properly secured in the boat to prevent excessive movement. All portable tanks should be filled on the **pier**. Close all **hatches** and other openings on the boat before fueling.

- **Anchor and Anchor Line.** All boats should be equipped with an adequate **anchor** chosen for the specific type of bottom encountered. The **line** should be of suitable size and length for the boat and depth of water. The anchor line should be five to ten times the water depth.

- **Backup Propulsion.**
  a. **Manual Propulsion.** A boater needs an auxiliary means of moving the boat if the engine isn't working. All boats less than 16 feet in length should carry alternate means of propulsion, such as oars or paddles.

  b. **Mechanical Propulsion.** If secondary mechanical propulsion is used (outboard or trolling motor), it should use a separate starting and fuel source from the main propulsion system.

- **Spare Parts.** To avoid being stranded in the event of a breakdown, carry spare parts, such as spark plugs, and a spare **propeller**.

- **Hull Repair.** Should the boat run **aground**, what would it take to repair a hole or crack in the hull? Repair kits, tapes and other packing materials that are applicable for temporary hull repair are readily available.

- **Bailers.** A boat should carry at least one effective manual bailer (dewatering device, i.e., bucket, can, scoop, etc.). This is in addition to any installed electric bilge pumps.

- **Miscellaneous Equipment.** Since the weather may change suddenly or an unforeseen circumstance may result in a boater being stranded, it is a good idea to pack miscellaneous equipment that will enhance personal comfort. A boater should consider such items as: binoculars, a VHF radio (if one is not installed on the boat), a **chart** and **compass**, **rope** and throw bag, foul weather gear, tool kit, first aid kit (which includes sunblock [SPF 15 or greater]), water, and perhaps some food.

Other items that might come in handy are extra clothing, watch, cap, gloves, sun hat, and sun glasses.

REVIEW EXERCISE: RECOMMENDED EQUIPMENT

1. Name at least four pieces of additional equipment a prudent boater should take along.
   1. _____
   2. _____
   3. _____
   4. _____

2. The length of the anchor line should be _____ to _____ times the depth of the water in which the boat is anchored.

3. In case of engine failure, secondary mechanical propulsion should run through the main propulsion fuel and starting source.
   ☐ True ☐ False

COURTESY MARINE EXAMINATION (CME)

As a public service, the United States Coast Guard Auxiliary (USCG Aux) will perform a Courtesy Marine Examination (CME). This free check of the boat and its equipment covers federal and state requirements, as well as additional USCG Auxiliary requirements. The check is conducted only when requested by the boat owner.

PIER: A loading/ landing platform extending at an angle from the shore.

HATCH: An opening in a boat's deck fitted with a watertight cover.

ANCHOR: A heavy metal device, fastened to chain or line, to hold a vessel in position, partly because of its weight, but chiefly because the designed shape digs into the bottom.

LINE: Rope and cordage used aboard a vessel.

PROPELLER: A rotating device with two or more blades that acts as a screw in propelling a vessel.

AGROUND: Touching or fast to the bottom.

CHART: A map for use by navigators.

COMPASS: Navigation instrument, either magnetic (showing magnetic north) or gyro (showing true north).

ROPE: Rope is called rope when purchased at a store. When it comes aboard a vessel and is put to use, it is called line.

If the boat meets all CME requirements, the owner will be awarded a CME seal (decal). If the boat does not pass, the owner is advised of the deficiencies noted. No report of these deficiencies is made to any law enforcement official. This examination is just another way of making sure the boat is "ship shape."

UNITED STATES COAST GUARD
COURTESY
U.S. COAST GUARD AUXILIARY
EXAMINATION

	Yes	No
◼ Personal Flotation Devices (PFDs)		
◼ Sound-Producing Devices		
◼ Bell - Boats 12m (39.4ft) or longer		
◼ Navigation Lights and Shapes		
◼ Fire Extinguishers		
◼ Visual Distress Signals		
◼ Inland		
◼ International		
◼ Ventilation		
◼ Backfire Flame Arrester		
◼ Fuel Systems		
◼ Anchor and Anchor Line		
◼ Alternate Propulsion		
◼ Dewatering Device		
◼ General Conditions		
◼ Overall Vessel Condition		
◼ Electrical System		
◼ Galley and Heating		
◼ Numbering		
◼ Registration/Documentation		
◼ State Requirements		
◼ Marine Sanitation Device		
◼ Pollution Placards		
◼ Navigation Rules		
◼ Special Decals (if required)		

SUMMARY
LEGAL REQUIREMENTS

This chapter covered the legal requirements for boaters. Requirements for boats are very similar to those for automobiles. Safety equipment needed on board varies depending on the length of the boat and on its power source. Other lessons learned:

- Federal and state laws require that boats be equipped with basic safety devices, such as Personal Flotation Devices (PFDs), fire extinguishers, proper ventilation systems and backfire flame arresters, and navigation lights.*

- If a boat is 16 feet or longer, each person on board must have a wearable PFD. Unless the boat is a canoe or kayak there must also be one throwable device (TYPE IV) aboard.

- By federal and state laws, all boats equipped with an engine must be numbered so they can be identified.

- Boats less than 39.4 feet must have some means of making an efficient sound signal.

- Visual Distress Signals (VDS) are required on all boats used on coastal waters, the Great Lakes, territorial seas, and those waters connected directly to them, inland to where a body of water is less than 2 miles wide.

- Navigation lights are required between sunset and sunrise, and during other periods of reduced visibility, such as fog, rain, haze, etc.

- To insure having the required equipment, request a free Courtesy Marine Examination (CME) from the USCG Auxiliary.

*See Preface

WHAT YOU WILL LEARN:
Informational Placards
MARPOL Annex V
Marine Sanitation Devices

Environmental Concerns

CHAPTER 3

INTRODUCTION

Upon completing this chapter, a boater should understand the problems associated with water pollution. Topics in this chapter include: water pollution, oil discharge, littering laws, waste management, and Marine Sanitation Devices (MSDs). It's important to remember that any pollution in the water ruins not only the aesthetic beauty, but also marine life. Pollution to fish and other marine life is like living with trash in your living room. REMEMBER: While you may be on the water to enjoy yourself, the fish are there to live.

Although pollution of the environment is a national concern, boaters working together can make a difference. Keep in mind that for any size boat, it is illegal to discharge or dump any substance into the water. This includes garbage, oil, and raw sewage.

WATER POLLUTION

As a result of an international conference on marine pollution, the U.S. Coast Guard announced that effective July 31, 1990, recreational boats over 26 feet in length must display a durably constructed informational placard which informs everyone on board of the rules and penalties governing the discharge of garbage at sea. Depending on the size of the boat, one or more placards are required.

In addition to the federal regulation, boaters should be aware of the state, regional and local restrictions that might apply.

Placards that comply with the regulations are available from marine supply shops and service stores.

DISCHARGE OF OIL

Vessels at least 26 feet in length must display a placard regarding the prohibition of oily discharge.

Discharge Of Oil Prohibited

The Federal Water Pollution Control Act prohibits the discharge of oil or oily waste into or upon the navigable waters of the United States or the waters of the contiguous zone if such discharge causes a film or sheen upon or a discoloration of the surface of the water or causes a sludge or emulsion beneath the surface of the water. Violators are subject to a penalty of $25,000.

Water Pollution Placard

It is illegal for any vessel to dump plastic trash anywhere in the ocean or navigable waters of the United States. Annex V of the MARPOL TREATY is a new International Law for a cleaner, safer marine environment. Each violation of these requirements may result in civil penalty up to $25,000, a fine up to $50,000, and imprisonment up to 5 years.

U.S. Lakes, Rivers, Bays, Sounds, and 3 miles from shore
ILLEGAL TO DUMP
Plastic & Garbage
Paper   Metal
Rags   Crockery
Glass   Dunnage
Food

3 to 12 miles
ILLEGAL TO DUMP
Plastic
Dunnage (lining & packing materials that float) also if not ground to less than one inch:
Paper   Crockery
Rags   Metal
Glass   Food

12 to 25 miles
ILLEGAL TO DUMP
Plastic
Dunnage (lining & packing materials that float)

Outside 25 miles
ILLEGAL TO DUMP
Plastic

State and local regulations may further restrict the disposal of garbage.

WORKING TOGETHER WE CAN ALL MAKE A DIFFERENCE!
CENTER FOR MARINE CONSERVATION 1725 DeSales Street, NW Washington, DC 20036 (202)429-5609

ILLEGAL TO DUMP

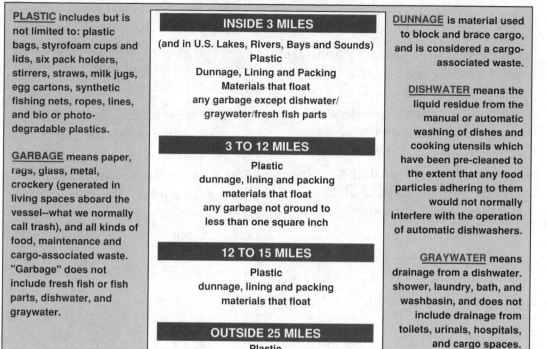

PLASTIC includes but is not limited to: plastic bags, styrofoam cups and lids, six pack holders, stirrers, straws, milk jugs, egg cartons, synthetic fishing nets, ropes, lines, and bio or photo-degradable plastics.

GARBAGE means paper, rags, glass, metal, crockery (generated in living spaces aboard the vessel--what we normally call trash), and all kinds of food, maintenance and cargo-associated waste. "Garbage" does not include fresh fish or fish parts, dishwater, and graywater.

INSIDE 3 MILES
(and in U.S. Lakes, Rivers, Bays and Sounds)
Plastic
Dunnage, Lining and Packing
Materials that float
any garbage except dishwater/
graywater/fresh fish parts

3 TO 12 MILES
Plastic
dunnage, lining and packing
materials that float
any garbage not ground to
less than one square inch

12 TO 15 MILES
Plastic
dunnage, lining and packing
materials that float

OUTSIDE 25 MILES
Plastic

DUNNAGE is material used to block and brace cargo, and is considered a cargo-associated waste.

DISHWATER means the liquid residue from the manual or automatic washing of dishes and cooking utensils which have been pre-cleaned to the extent that any food particles adhering to them would not normally interfere with the operation of automatic dishwashers.

GRAYWATER means drainage from a dishwater. shower, laundry, bath, and washbasin, and does not include drainage from toilets, urinals, hospitals, and cargo spaces.

Littering Laws

IT IS ILLEGAL FOR ANY VESSEL TO DUMP PLASTIC TRASH ANYWHERE IN THE OCEAN OR NAVIGABLE WATERS OF THE UNITED STATES

LITTERING LAWS

Every boat 26 feet or more in length and operating on federal waters is required to post, in a prominent place for everyone on board to see, a placard detailing all disposal prohibitions.

For more information on these requirements, call the U.S.C.G. Customer Infoline 1-800-368-5647.

WASTE MANAGEMENT

The Regulations for the Prevention of Pollution by Garbage from Ships, found in Annex V of MARPOL 73/78, require that vessels 40 feet or more in length must have waste management plans (see below).

U.S.C.G. Customer Infoline

U.S. Department of Transportation

United States Coast Guard

1-800-368-5647

Call Toll Free for Information

Produced by the U.S. Coast Guard Boating Education Branch 3/1/92

- To receive information on boating safety recalls.
- To report possible defects on boats.
- To comment on U.S.C.G. boarding procedures.
- To inquire about boating safety.
- To request boating safety literature.

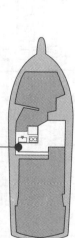

Waste Management Plan
for the Chelsea Marie
NOTICE TO ALL HANDS

- All Garbage will be placed in trash can in the galley.

- Under no circumstance will any trash be dumped over the side without notifying the captain of the **CHELSEA MARIE.**

- When trash can is full, replace the trash bag and put the full trash bag in the stern area of the vessel.

- All trash will be dumped in the dumpster at the marina.

- The captain of the CHELSEA MARIE is responsible to insure the plan is carried out.

3•3

MARINE SANITATION DEVICES (MSDs)

Installed toilets that are not equipped with Marine Sanitation Devices (MSDs), and discharge raw sewage directly over the sides, are illegal. Boats are not required to be equipped with toilets or marine **heads**. However, if a toilet is installed, it must be equipped with an operable MSD that is built and certified to meet Coast Guard standards.

As of January 30, 1980, if a boat has a toilet or head installed, it must be equipped with an operable MSD. Vessels 65 feet in length and under may install a device that treats the sewage with disinfectant chemicals, or other means, before it is discharged into the water. The treated discharge must meet certain health standards for bacterial content and must not show any visible floating solids.

An MSD must have a certification label affixed that shows the name of the manufacturer, the name and model number of the device, the month and year of manufacture, the MSD type, a certification number, and a certification statement.

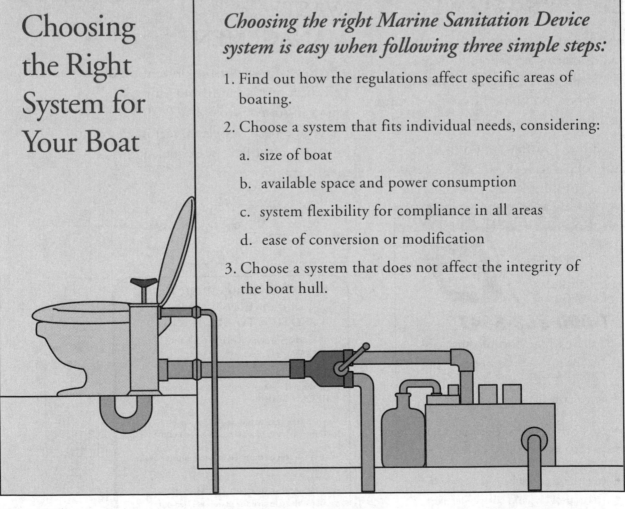

MARINE SANITATION SYSTEM

Choosing the Right System for Your Boat

Choosing the right Marine Sanitation Device system is easy when following three simple steps:

1. Find out how the regulations affect specific areas of boating.

2. Choose a system that fits individual needs, considering:

   a. size of boat

   b. available space and power consumption

   c. system flexibility for compliance in all areas

   d. ease of conversion or modification

3. Choose a system that does not affect the integrity of the boat hull.

SUMMARY

ENVIRONMENTAL CONCERNS

There are laws and regulations which govern the disposal of garbage, plastics, oil and sewage. Remember to display the appropriate placard and to use the proper Marine Sanitation Devices.

GIVE A HOOT, DON'T POLLUTE.

Weather CHAPTER 4

INTRODUCTION

The environment is going to be a primary concern to every skipper who operates a vessel which has no brakes on a "road" which moves and has various hazards and conditions that may change with relation to the weather. The first step in planning a boat trip is to check the weather and weather forecasts. As the skipper, you will be interested in knowing what the weather is at your current location, what it is where you are going, as well as what the weather is expected to be while you are out on the water. An awareness of the weather, as well as where to find this information, is an important survival factor.

A knowledge of weather data sources is important; however, reviewing weather

4•1

forecasts is not enough. Monitoring weather conditions throughout the day is necessary to supplement limited weather information.

PREPARATION AND PLANNING

Local Newspaper

Read the entire report, not just the summary. A good idea is to tear the report out of the paper and take it along. Make sure it applies to specific locations and waters.

The National Weather Service

This service publishes Coastal Warning Facilities Charts for all coastal areas, which state the locations and phone numbers of all National Weather Service offices plus the location and times of AM and FM radio and television marine weather broadcasts.

National Oceanic and Atmospheric Administration (NOAA) Weather Radio Broadcasts

Weather reports updated each hour (VHF-FM channels WX-1, 162.550 MHz; WX-2, 162.400 MHz; WX-3, 162.475 MHz; WX-4, 162.425 MHz; WX-5, 162.450 MHz; WX-6, 162.500 MHz; or WX-7, 162.525 MHz). Channel selection is dependent upon the area of operation. For more information write to National Weather Service, Attn: (W/OM 11), National Oceanic and Atmospheric Administration, Silver Spring, MD 20910. As a helpful hint, consider keeping an AM radio on. Increase in static and volume of static may indicate a storm moving into the area.

United States Coast Guard

The Coast Guard also broadcasts special marine weather information, including small craft advisories, on VHF Channel 22. Visual warnings are no longer operated by the National Weather Service. However, certain organizations continue to display lights and flags when rough weather is expected.

Weather Channel

Television and Cable Television are good sources of information.

WEATHER HAZARDS

Lightning

Thunderstorms can be dangerous because they produce lightning in addition to strong winds and rough seas. Lightning is a huge spark of static electricity which is generated from electric charges built up within cumulonimbus clouds and the ground.

Cumulonimbus Clouds

Minimize the danger of having a boat struck by lightning by following a few basic safety principles and exercising common sense. If caught in open water, seek shelter (marina, etc.). If trapped on the water during a thunderstorm, stay low in the middle of the boat and stay away from grounded fittings. Installing a grounding system on the boat may also be helpful, but is not always sufficient to prevent damage or fire. Basically, this system requires a high capacity electrical conductor to be run from the highest point on the boat in a straight vertical line to a submerged ground plate, or to an exposed metal keel.

Downbursts

There have been numerous reports of the effects of "wind shear" on aircraft during takeoffs or landings. A similar phenomenon may also occur on the water and affect boats. Caused by thunderstorms, these localized, strong winds are called DOWNBURSTS. Although there are several ways in which these winds form, they all

exhibit certain characteristics: 1) winds may exceed 130 mph - much faster than even the normally gusty thunderstorm winds, 2) the strong winds hit suddenly with little or no warning, and 3) the strongest winds affect a relatively small area.

DOWNBURSTS come from thunderstorms. Therefore, whenever a boater encounters a thunderstorm, a DOWNBURST is possible. This is true if the thunderstorm is isolated or is part of a series, such as a squall line.

When a DOWNBURST first strikes the surface, it is often concentrated in an area less than three miles across. This is generally where the most extreme winds can be found. The term MICROBURST is often used in describing this phase. After striking the ground, the winds begin to spread out, eventually covering an area up to 30 or 40 miles across. However,

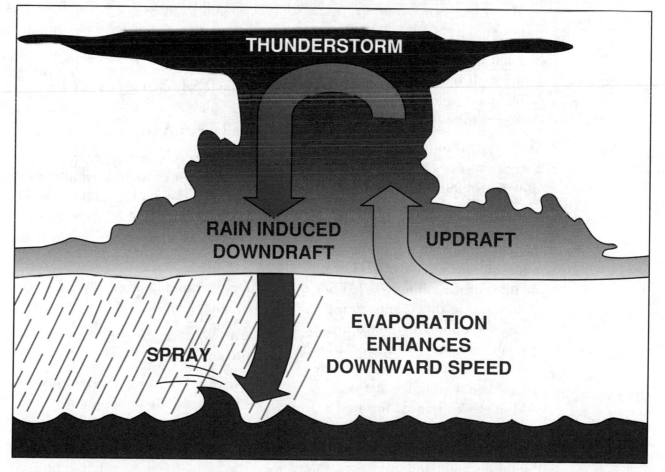

MICROBURSTS can still be embedded in the general DOWNBURST.

DOWNBURSTS are usually short-lived high winds lasting only a few minutes. However, one thunderstorm can produce a series of these winds affecting a swath several miles long and lasting an hour or more.

DOWNBURSTS hit so rapidly that few signs may be available to alert the boater as to their presence. Blowing spray under or slightly ahead of a thunderstorm may be the only indicator. However, the best rule is, avoid ALL thunderstorms if possible. If not, expect and prepare for the worst whenever a thunderstorm is encountered.

The hazards of Downbursts are:

- Extreme, sudden winds which can tip a sailboat beyond its range of upright stability

- Heavy seas that can capsize powerboats

- High winds that can blow equipment off the deck and cause persons on board to lose balance and fall overboard

Boats caught out on open water under these conditions can encounter a downburst without expecting it. DOWNBURSTS are generally short-lived, lasting only a few minutes. This fact makes predicting their occurrence almost an impossible task. The sudden loss of the sailing vessel "Pride of Baltimore" in the Atlantic near Puerto Rico in 1986 was attributed to a downburst wind. Witnesses claim in less than two minutes, the ship blew over, filled with water, and sank. Although this tragedy involved a larger sailing vessel on the open ocean, similar dangers have been experienced by vessels on inland or inshore waters.

Thunderstorms

Thunderstorms can create several downbursts in succession, with varying degrees of intensity. A thunderstorm might even generate a combination of downbursts and tornadoes, or smaller versions known as "water spouts" or "whirlwinds."

Protection During a Thunderstorm

- Turn the craft with the bow heading into the wind, and reef the sails, if on a sailboat. These actions help minimize wind resistance. Sailboats with mechanical power should drop all sails and "motor" out of the wind.

- Secure all loose objects and rigging on-deck, and make certain hatches or other openings are covered.

- Wear a personal flotation device, making sure it fits securely. Keep other lifesaving equipment readily accessible, including inflatable rafts, visual distress signals, throw ropes, and man-overboard markers.

STORM WARNINGS

Small Craft Advisory:

Small Craft Advisory is generally associated with sustained winds 18 to 33 **knots**, or waves hazardous to small boats. Small Craft Advisories are not issued during the winter months along the Great Lakes.

Gale Warning: (Sustained winds 34 to 47 knots)

Storm Warning: (Sustained winds 48 knots or more)

Hurricane Warning: (Sustained winds 64 knots or more associated with a hurricane)

Special Marine Warning: (Winds of 35 knots or more lasting generally less than two hours. These are usually associated with an individual thunderstorm or an organized series of thunderstorms [squall line, cold front].)

REVIEW EXERCISE:
WEATHER

1. The basic question to consider concerning weather is, "Is it safe to _____ out on the water?"

2. List two prevailing sources of weather information.

   _____

   _____

3. Increased static on the AM radio could mean _____.

4. Minimize the danger of lightning striking the boat by installing a _____ system with a high capacity _____.

5. To be protected in a downburst, the skipper should orient the boat with the _____ facing _____ the wind.

SUMMARY
WEATHER

Even though it is not always possible to predict the weather, checking marine radio stations or newspapers will help the skipper. The skipper should always call to find out what the forecast is prior to planning a boat trip.

When out on the water, be careful of lightning and downbursts. If there is lightning — get off the water!

During downbursts, orient the craft with the bow facing the wind, secure loose objects and have everyone on board wear a PFD.

Before You Go

CHAPTER 5

INTRODUCTION

The weather forecast provides valuable information about water conditions. Indeed, a foul weather forecast may cause a cancellation of the planned trip. Fortunately, there are several sources to obtain weather information, including the newspaper, television, radio, and marine radio broadcast.

Whether you're boating for a few hours or a few days, there are "safety" procedures to follow. This chapter explains several safety procedures, such as filing a float plan, checking equipment, loading the boat, and fueling the boat. These procedures are important because the skipper is ultimately responsible for passenger safety.

FILING THE FLOAT PLAN

There are two procedures to follow before leaving home. The first is to check the weather. The second is to file a float plan and give it to a responsible person. At a minimum, a float plan should include, **when** you are departing, **where** you are going, **when** you plan to return, and **who** you have with you. The plan should also include a description of the boat (including name and registration number) and other pertinent information which could help identify the vessel. *(See APPENDIX G)*

The float plan makes assistance possible should anything occur (such as running out of gas, running aground, or worse). Although the Coast Guard does not have the facilities to hold the float plan, the Coast Guard serves as Search and Rescue (SAR) coordinator for all maritime emergencies and is the appropriate point of contact by the person holding the float plan. In a similar fashion, for inland recreational boating, the local county sheriff, police or rescue squad could serve as the appropriate point of contact by the person holding the float plan. Advise the person holding the float plan who to contact in case of emergency. Stick to the float plan when on the water, so any rescue group will know where to find the boat if necessary.

NOTE: Don't forget to notify the person holding the float plan that the return trip has been completed or altered.

REVIEW EXERCISE: FLOAT PLAN

1. The four W's of the float plan are:

W_____ you are departing.

W_____ you are going.

W_____ you are coming back.

W_____ you have with you.

2. A Float Plan should be filed with _____.

3. If there is concern for the boater's safety, the holder of the Float Plan should contact _____.

CHECKING EQUIPMENT

Check to be sure equipment is ready, accessible and in working order. This will not take long, and should be a regular part of your pre-departure planning. Make it a regular boating safety habit. Consider making a checklist that you can use each time in preparation for your boating activity.

First, is the transom <u>plug</u> in the boat?

Second, check the <u>Personal Flotation Devices</u> (PFDs), also known as "life jackets." Are they USCG Approved? Are they in good condition? Are they easily accessible? Make sure everyone in the boat sees them and knows how to put them on. Have all passengers aboard try on their PFDs and adjust them for proper fit. Check the straps — be sure they're secure and not torn. A short PFD use drill with passengers is good practice, especially if the passengers have never worn PFDs before.

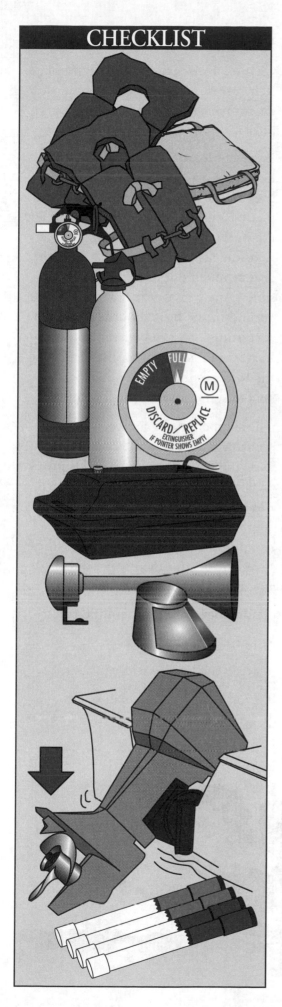

CHECKLIST

Third, are <u>Fire Extinguishers</u> aboard? Are they USCG Approved? Are they easily accessible? Are they in the proper rack or clamp? Can they be quickly removed for use? Is the clamp frozen with rust? Do the passengers know where to locate them and how to use them? Have the pressure gauges been checked to make sure they are fully charged and ready to use? Are the safety pins free to remove? As previously noted, don't test the extinguishers by pressing the start lever; the valve may not reset afterwards, rendering the unit inoperable.

Fourth, <u>Fuel Tanks</u>. Are all portable fuel tanks stowed properly? Are they in good condition? Are the covers on tight? Is all spillage wiped up? Are the hoses connected properly to tank and engine (for outboards)? Have fuel lines been checked for leaks?

Fifth, <u>Lights and Horn</u>. This is an easy, quick check. Just try them out briefly. Are there spare fuses and spare lamps (bulbs)? Is there a bell, plastic whistle, or hand-operated horn in case the power horn fails?

Sixth, <u>Engine</u>. Is the engine down and locked (for outboards)? Is it set at the proper angle for the load in the boat? Are the fuel hoses connected tightly? Are the steering cables connected and tested? Is the ignition key on board?

Seventh, <u>Distress Signals</u>. Are Visual Distress Signals (VDS) dry and ready to use?

Last, but not least, <u>Auxiliary Equipment</u> — (not a legal requirement). As noted in Chapter 2, such additional equipment should include portable fuel tanks, anchor and anchor line, backup propulsion (manual and/or mechanical), spare parts, hull repair material, bailers, and miscellaneous equipment (first aid kit, binoculars, and extra clothing).

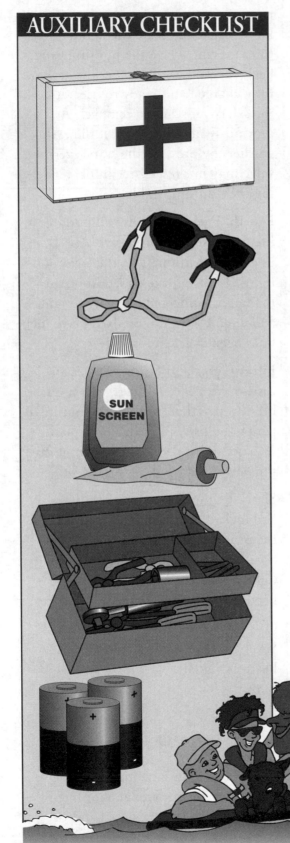

AUXILIARY CHECKLIST

LOADING THE BOAT

Chapter 1 discussed the capacity plate. Remember, the capacity plate helps to determine the number of people a boat will hold safely (the load).

Now let's look at where and how to load the boat. After fueling, tie the boat to the pier. Have people on the pier pass gear to the individual loading the boat. Keep the load low and see that it is distributed evenly. Stow the gear as much out of the way as possible. Any heavy gear that might slide around in the boat should be secured. A shifting load can be hazardous to boaters. In addition to distributing the load evenly, do not allow passengers to stand up in a small boat.

The skipper enters the boat first, securing the gear in the boat and allowing passengers, with PFDs properly fastened, to step into the boat, one at a time. The passengers should step in carefully. They should not jump into the boat. The smaller the boat, the greater the danger of capsizing when entering the boat.

Remember these four simple rules:

- Distribute the load evenly.

- Keep the load low in the boat.

- Don't stand up in small boats.

- Never overload.

FUELING

Fueling the boat should be done very carefully. A number of serious accidents occur each year due to gasoline explosions and fires. Nearly all were due to the skipper's failure to observe simple precautions.

There are **five common sense rules** to apply when fueling. Learn them and follow them.

1. Always fuel the boat in good light. Portable tanks must be removed from the boat for filling.

2. When the boat is tied up at a fueling dock:

   a. Don't smoke, light matches or lighters, or operate electric switches.

   b. Stop engines, motors, fans — anything that might cause a spark.

   c. Secure all fires. Don't forget the pilot light on gas stoves and gas-operated portable refrigerators.

3. Before fueling:

   a. Make certain that the boat is well secured to the pier or wharf. Get everyone out of the boat.

   b. Close ports, windows, doors and hatches to keep the vapor out of the boat.

   c. Check tanks, filler pipes, tank vents, and flame screens.

   d. Check to see how much fuel the tank will take.

4. During fueling:

   a. Keep the nozzle of the hose in contact with the tank opening to prevent static sparks.

   b. Guard against spillage, if fuel spills, wipe it up immediately. Don't let any liquid get below.

Keep fuel nozzle in contact with tank opening at all times to prevent static sparks.

5. After fueling:

   a. Replace caps (covers) of fill openings.

   b. Open up the boat completely and ventilate.

   c. Air out the boat for at least five minutes.

   d. Give all low spots (engine bilges, tank spaces) the sniff test. If gasoline vapor is detected, continue to air out the boat, look for spillage and leaks.

   e. Wipe up all spills.

REVIEW EXERCISE:

FUELING

1. Fill all portable tanks

   _____ .

2. Before fueling, the skipper should _____

   and stop _____ .

3. During fueling, keep the nozzle of the hose_____

   _____ .

SUMMARY

BEFORE YOU GO

Filing a float plan aids and protects the boater in emergency situations. Even though many times the objective of boating is to be left alone to enjoy the solitude and beauty of the area, the float plan is important. A responsible and dependable person should hold the float plan, which should include departure, destination, and return information. This plan is written "just in case" and is for the boater's protection.

Also, before getting underway, check the equipment. Check for required PFDs, fire extinguishers, fuel tanks, VDS, etc.

Carefully filling a boat with fuel is important. Turn off engines, don't smoke, get everyone away, and clean up leaks.

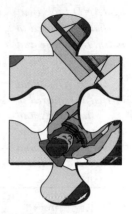

Basic Navigation Rules

CHAPTER 6

INTRODUCTION

With fishing boats, sailboats, commercial boats, powerboats, canoes, tow boats and personal watercraft, the waterways are more crowded than ever before! Therefore, all boaters need to understand basic navigation, aids to navigation, charts, dead reckoning, and rules of the road.

This chapter will identify operating procedures, signals and lights as found in the Navigational Rules book *(shown on page 6-2)*.

The Navigation Rules were established to provide guidance to boat operators on steering and sailing rules, lights, sound signals and other general protocol for safe navigation. For further information regarding

"Navigation Rules: International-Inland," (COMDTINST M1667.2C), contact:

Superintendent of Documents
U.S. Government Printing Office
P.O. Box 371954
Pittsburgh, PA 15250-7954

If a boat is at least 12 meters (39.37 feet) in length and operating on federal waters, a copy of the INLAND RULES (only when operating in inland waters) must be on board.

The INLAND RULES generally apply to internal U.S. waters. The INTERNATIONAL RULES apply to those areas found outside the demarcation lines contained in the NAVRULES book.

RULES OF THE ROAD

These situations, signals and actions are based on the INLAND NAVIGATION RULES.

The Navigation Rules were written with the intention of PREVENTING collisions, not to give one boat the right of way over another. The RESPONSIBILITY for preventing collisions rests with BOTH vessels. Whenever possible, maneuver as necessary to avoid an accident. Remember, don't be dead right!

Two terms to be familiar with are "**Stand On**" and "**Give Way**." The "Stand On" boat is the one required to maintain course and speed. The "Give Way" vessel is the one required to take early and substantial action to keep well clear and avoid a collision.

On shore, an automobile signalling with a directional light or hand signal indicates the driver's intention to pass or turn. The purpose is to make certain the other drivers know the intent of the vehicle so they won't take some action that might cause an accident. On the water, an item such as a whistle or horn is used to signal the skipper's INTENTION.

There are three types of situations between two boats where whistle signals should be given: meeting, crossing and overtaking.

The length of the blasts is part of the signalling code. A prolonged blast lasts from 4-6 seconds. A short blast is about one second in duration.

- One short blast means "I intend to pass you on my port side."

- One prolonged blast is the signal that a power-driven boat is leaving a dock or berth.

- Two short blasts mean "I intend to pass you on my starboard side."

- Three short blasts means "I am operating astern propulsion."

- Five or more short blasts is the signal for danger.

When meeting head-on or nearly so, stay to the right. If necessary, one boat gives a single short blast; the other RESPONDS with the same signal. Now each skipper knows what the other is going to do and each one has confirmed it.

When two boats meet passing starboard to starboard, two short blasts are given and the other skipper should respond with two short blasts.

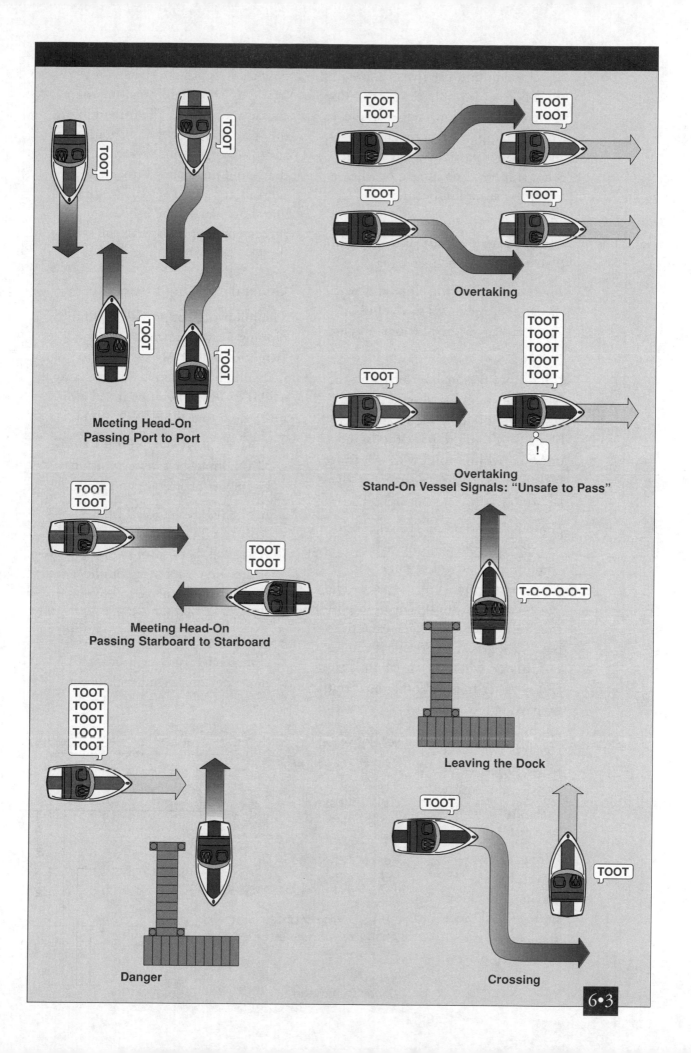

If at any time there is confusion about signals or intent, use five or more short blasts. It's only prudent to stop if there is confusion. For example, this can happen when one boat gives an improper passing signal and the other skipper is confused, or when the following situation occurs:

"BOAT-A is backing away from the dock and may not see BOAT-B, who then sounds the danger signal?"

There are overtaking situations when the skipper may pass the "stand on" vessel either on the port or starboard side.

If it's more reasonable to pass on the "stand on" boat's starboard (right), signal the intention with one short blast. If it's safe to pass, the "stand on" boat will respond with one short blast. The one short blast reply gives the go ahead.

Should the "stand on" vessel consider it unsafe to pass as requested, the "stand on" boat will respond with five short blasts (the danger signal). The "give way" boat must remain in position and make no further attempt to pass. The passing agreement can be re-initiated when the situation is clear. If it is easier to avoid other boat traffic by passing left, the appropriate sound signal is two short blasts. After hearing the same reply, it is permissible to proceed.

When a power-driven boat is leaving a dock or berth, the skipper shall sound one prolonged blast.

Finally, in a crossing situation, the boat to the starboard (right) is the "stand on" boat and must maintain course and speed. The other boat is the "give way" vessel and should slow and/or change course to cross behind the "stand on" boat. Either skipper can initiate sound signals by giving one short blast. The other, if in agreement, responds with the same signal — one short blast.

General Yielding Order

The following list provides a simple ranking of who normally has the "Right of Way." Always yield to boats with a higher ranking. As an example, a SAILBOAT, when under sail alone, must yield to a FISHING BOAT.

1. A VESSEL NOT UNDER COMMAND may be a vessel which has lost power or steerage and is adrift.

2. A VESSEL RESTRICTED IN ABILITY TO MANEUVER is a vessel that, because of its work (such as dredging, surveying, or underwater operations), is unable to keep out of the way of another vessel.

3. A FISHING VESSEL refers to commercial fishermen towing or dragging equipment, such as nets.

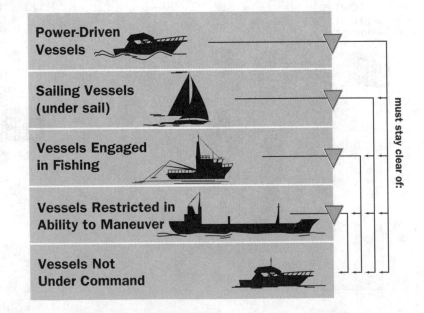

Power-Driven Vessels

Sailing Vessels (under sail)

Vessels Engaged in Fishing

Vessels Restricted in Ability to Maneuver

Vessels Not Under Command

must stay clear of:

4. A SAILING VESSEL, when under sail alone, is limited in its maneuverability because it uses the wind for propulsion.

5. A POWER-DRIVEN VESSEL. Exceptions: VESSEL overtaking

(RULE 3), vessels in narrow channels (RULE 9) and traffic separation services (RULE 10).

NOTE: These rules are found in Navigation Rules International-Inland.

REVIEW EXERCISE:

RULES OF THE ROAD

Inland rules apply to the following situations.

1. Boats A and B are on course as shown. Boat A sounds _____ short blast(s). Boat B replies with _____ short blast(s).

2. Here Boats A and B are meeting head on. What signals do they exchange and what course changes do they make?

_____

_____

3. In this situation:

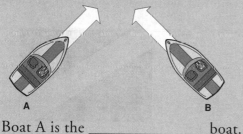

Boat A is the _____ boat.

Boat B is the _____ boat.

What must Boat A do?

_____

What must Boat B do?

_____

4. In this case Boat A is overtaking Boat B and wishes to pass Boat B on Boat B's right side.

Boat A is the _____ boat.

Boat B is the _____ boat.

Boat A sounds _____ short blast(s).

Boat B sounds _____ short blast(s).

5. Shown below is another overtaking situation. Boat B wishes to pass Boat A on Boat A's left side. However, Boat A sees a potentially dangerous condition ahead that Boat B may not see.

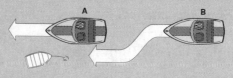

Boat B sounds _____ short blast(s).

Boat A sounds _____ short blast(s).

What does Boat B do now?

_____

_____

RESTRICTED VISIBILITY

Whenever fog, rain, snow, smoke, or any other phenomena reduce the ability to see (or be seen), sound signals should be used. General rules to follow are:

1. Power-driven boats underway and moving through the water shall sound one prolonged (4-6 seconds) blast at not more than two-minute intervals.

2. A power-driven boat underway, but stopped and not moving, shall sound two prolonged blasts in succession, in not more than two-minute intervals.

3. Sailboats under sail should sound three blasts in succession; one prolonged, then two short, at not more than two-minute intervals.

4. A boat at anchor sounds a rapid ringing of the bell for five seconds at one-minute intervals.

NOTE: A boat less than 12 meters (39.37 feet) at anchor does not have to give this signal. However, some effective signal should be given at not more than two-minute intervals.

Lights Used When Anchored

Power boats and sailboats at anchor must display anchor lights (all around white light). However, boats less than 7 meters (23.0 feet) in length are not required to display them unless anchored in or near a narrow channel, fairway or anchorage, or where other boats normally navigate.

An anchor light for a boat less than 50 meters (164.0 feet) in length is an all around white light, visible for two miles, and exhibited where it can best be seen.

A boat less than 20 meters (65.6 feet) in length, when at anchor in a SPECIAL ANCHORAGE AREA, is not required to exhibit an anchor light. SPECIAL anchorage areas are away from the main flow of boat traffic and located where general navigation will not endanger or be endangered by unlighted vessels.

DIVING OPERATIONS

The Navigation Rules require small vessels engaged in diving operations to show a rigid replica of the international code flag "A". This requirement doesn't have any impact on the use of the red and white diver's flag, which may be required by state or local law or used by choice to mark the diver's location. The "A" alpha-flag is a navigation signal advertising only the operation in which the boat is engaged. It doesn't pertain to the diver.

Diving

Diving is a rapidly growing sport and much of it takes place in areas of recreational boating. While operating a boat, keep a sharp lookout for divers. Some dive from a boat while others swim out from shore. Divers will usually display the flag shown below.

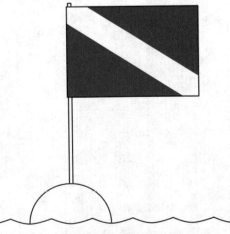

Diver Down Flag

Sometimes this flag is attached to a small floating buoy or an inflated innertube. When divers are operating from a boat, and that boat is restricted in its ability to maneuver, the Navigation Rules require it to display a rigid replica of the international code flag "A" not less than one meter (3.3 feet) in height (when it is impractical to show the shapes otherwise required for vessels restricted in their ability to maneuver). See the sketch below. Be aware that the "A" flag is a navigation signal advertising the boat's restricted condition.

The flag shown below does not pertain to the diver as the commonly used red and white diver's flag does. IN ALL CASES stay well clear and watch for swimmers, snorkelers and/or air bubbles in the water. Slow down and be prepared to stop the engine instantly. Learn to identify and know what to do when the flags are displayed.

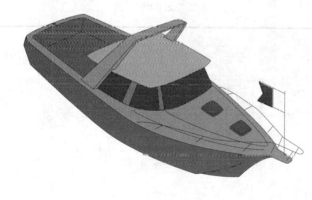

"A" Alpha Flag

Special Zone Areas

Just like the diver's flag, there are other zoned areas which are restricted. For example, study this symbol for a moment.

This symbol may appear on a buoy, signboard, or flag. Its meaning is simple: it's an area reserved for swimmers and boats are to STAY OUT! This symbol may also mean, DAM, WATERFALL, RAPIDS, etc. and in general means BOATS KEEP OUT! STAY CLEAR!

SUMMARY

BASIC NAVIGATION

This chapter stressed that the book "Navigation Rules: International-Inland," provides guidelines for boat operation. Three other essential points for the skipper were:

- taking precautions when visibility is restricted,

- using lights when the boat is anchored,

- and recognizing and displaying proper flags when diving operations are conducted.

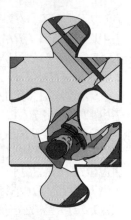

WHAT YOU WILL LEARN:

Two Systems

Hazards Around Dams

Aids to Navigation

CHAPTER 7

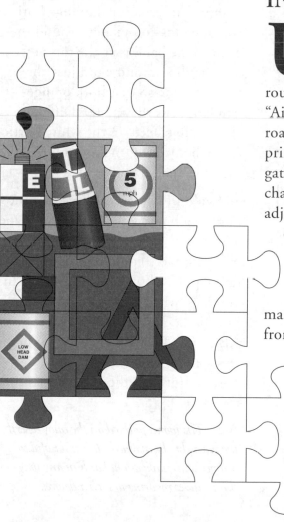

INTRODUCTION

Unlike the roads and highways, waterways do not have signs that tell the location, the route, or the distance to a destination. "Aids to Navigation" (ATON) are the road signs of the waterways. The primary objective of the aids to navigation system is to mark navigable channels and waterways, obstructions adjacent to these waterways, and obstructions in areas of general navigation which may not be anticipated. Other waters, even if navigable, are generally not marked. Navigation Aids can range from a single rock pile with a sign affixed to it, to an array of visible, audible, and electronic signals. Navigational aids are placed at various points along the coasts, rivers, lakes, channels and harbors, as

NOTE: ALL AIDS TO NAVIGATION ARE PROTECTED BY LAW. IT'S A CRIMINAL OFFENSE TO CAUSE ANY DAMAGE OR HINDRANCE TO THE PROPER OPERATION OF AN AID. DO NOT ALTER, DEFACE, MOVE OR DESTROY ANY AID TO NAVIGATION. NEVER TIE A BOAT TO A BUOY, DAYBEACON OR LIGHT STRUCTURE. AVOID ANCHORING SO CLOSE TO AN AID THAT THE AID IS OBSTRUCTED (HIDDEN) FROM THE SIGHT OF ANOTHER BOAT. REPORT ALL INTENTIONAL OR UNINTENTIONAL COLLISIONS WITH NAVIGATIONAL AIDS TO THE COAST GUARD.

markers and guides to help locate a position with respect to the shore and hidden dangers.

UNIFORM STATE WATERWAY MARKING SYSTEM (USWMS)

The Uniform State Waterway Marking System (USWMS) will be of major interest to the skippers who trailer boats to various lakes and streams.

This system was developed in 1966 to provide an easily understood system for operators of small boats. While designed for use on lakes and other inland waterways that are not portrayed on nautical charts, the USWMS was authorized for use on other waters as well. It supplements the existing federal marking system and is generally compatible with it.

Keep in mind that the conventional direction of buoyage is considered upstream or towards the head of a navigable waterway.

The USWMS varies from the Standard U.S. system as follows:

1) The color black is used instead of green.

2) There are three aids to navigation which reflect major significance:

a. A white buoy with red top represents an obstruction and the buoy should be passed to the south or west.

b. A white buoy with black top represents an obstruction and the buoy should be passed to the north or east.

c. A red and white vertically striped buoy indicates that an obstruction exists between that buoy and the nearest shore.

3) Mooring buoys are white buoys with a horizontal blue band midway between the waterline and the top of the buoy. The buoy may be lighted and will generally show a slow flashing white light.

Regulatory Markers

Regulatory markers are colored white with two international orange horizontal bands completely around the buoy. One band is at the top of the buoy with a second band just above the waterline so that both orange bands are clearly visible. Different shapes are placed on the white portion of the buoy body and are colored international orange.

Shown on Plate 1 in the back of the book is a buoy with a diamond shape which always means "DANGER," meaning there could be a dam, waterfall, rapids, or swimmers near by. In any case, when the diamond shape includes a cross, it means BOATS KEEP OUT! STAY CLEAR! Whether this symbol appears on a buoy, signpost and/or flag, the meaning is still the same.

Note: The words painted on the buoy describe the hazard to be avoided. It is unlawful to tamper with navigational aids in any way — this includes mooring to such a device!!

Another symbol is the circle, which indicates a control. These can also be placed on signboards ashore.

The lower left buoy shown above means STAY OUT.

Finally, a square or rectangle outlined in bright orange gives some form of piloting information.

LATERAL SYSTEM

The Lateral System is a system of aids to navigation in which characteristics of buoys and beacons indicate the sides of the channel or route relative to a conventional direction of buoyage (usually upstream).

Buoys

The illustration to the left depicts a CAN BUOY. It is so named because of its cylinder-like shape. CAN BUOYS are green. This type of buoy is found marking the left side of the channel when returning from a large body of water or when heading upstream and is often used to mark obstructions. It always has an ODD number, 1, 3, 5, and so on.

Can Buoys

From time to time a CAN BUOY painted in red and green bands may be seen. It won't have numbers on it, but may be LETTERED. This buoy marks the junction of two channels. The top color and the shape identifies which side of the buoy should be taken for the preferred (most used) route. Green on top (can buoy) — go to starboard (right), red on top (nun buoy) — go to port (left) when heading upstream.

Nun Buoys

The buoy to the left is known as a NUN buoy because of its shape.

Most NUN buoys are painted red with EVEN numbers - 2, 4, 6, etc. NUN buoys mark the right side of the channel, when returning from a large body of water or heading upstream.

Other NUN buoys may be painted with horizontal red and green bands. Like banded CAN buoys, these buoys also mark channel junctions.

Lighted Aids

The buoy shown here is a LIGHTED buoy. It may have any of the specified (red and white striped, red, or green) coloring which defines its meaning.

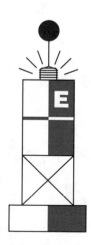

7•3

The red and white vertically striped buoy is a "center channel" or "safe water" aid. It may have a light, a radar reflector, bell, gong or whistle, so it is easily located in times of low visibility. It may also be lettered. The light will be the same color as the buoy. In the case of a red and white vertically striped buoy, the light will be white.

An aid to navigation is placed and its identifying characteristics chosen to mark the safe channel when entering from a large body of water or heading up stream. Many skippers remember this rule by memorizing the three "R's" or RED, RIGHT, RETURNING.

Channel Markers

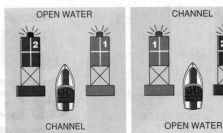

When leaving port and going out to sea (any open body of water), do the opposite. On lakes, going from the outlet of the lake to its upper end is the same as entering from the sea.

A word of caution: don't regard buoys as immovable objects. They may be missing or drifting from their proper position because of storms, tides or collisions. Learn to read charts correctly and report any buoy that is not properly located to the local U.S. Coast Guard Station or State Official.

Beacons

A permanent structure is a BEACON (sometimes referred to as a DAYBEACON or DAYBOARD). These structures exhibit a DAYMARK (sometimes referred to as a MARKER) The colors and shapes of the marker are identical to those found on CAN

and NUN buoys. The markers, however, are not floating in the water, but are affixed to poles. The same rules apply: port side, green, ODD numbers; and starboard side, red, EVEN numbers.

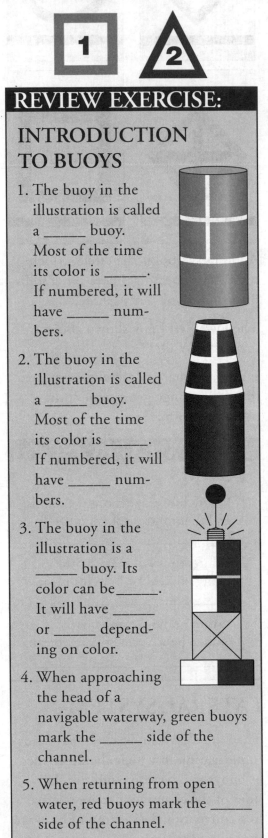

REVIEW EXERCISE:

INTRODUCTION TO BUOYS

1. The buoy in the illustration is called a _____ buoy. Most of the time its color is _____. If numbered, it will have _____ numbers.

2. The buoy in the illustration is called a _____ buoy. Most of the time its color is _____. If numbered, it will have _____ numbers.

3. The buoy in the illustration is a _____ buoy. Its color can be_____. It will have _____ or _____ depending on color.

4. When approaching the head of a navigable waterway, green buoys mark the _____ side of the channel.

5. When returning from open water, red buoys mark the _____ side of the channel.

Hazardous Areas

While some skippers may never operate a boat near a dam, others may. Everyone should be aware of the hazards involved. Areas immediately above and below dams are very dangerous to the safety of small boats; therefore, boats MUST STAY CLEAR. Observe and obey all signs and instructions. At dams where there is an open spillway, a boat that gets too close could be trapped and swept over the dam. If the dam is part of a hydro-electric power plant, there may be areas of extreme water turbulence just below the dam. Very often these power plants operate on a "demand" basis. That is, there may be perfectly calm water just below the dam — suddenly somebody opens a valve and a raging torrent of water pours forth that would capsize any boat. Even people wearing PFDs could be dragged under the surface of the water and drowned.

Intracoastal Waterway Aids

The aids to navigation on the Intracoastal Waterway are similar to the LATERAL system with an additional yellow border or band to signify the aid applies to the Intracoastal Waterway. Some aids apply to both a normal inlet from the sea and the Intracoastal Waterway. In this case the intracoastal skipper would use the yellow aid shape painted on the sea aid and ignore the shape of the aid while the seaway skipper would ignore the yellow marks and be guided by the basic aid color and shape. This combination can result in a can buoy being used as a nun (and the reverse) by the intracoastal skipper. Just remember that users of the Intracoastal Waterway use the aids with yellow and use the shape of the yellow marking instead of the shape of the aid.

Western River Aids

Aids to navigation on the Mississippi River, its tributaries, and certain other rivers which flow toward the gulf of Mexico (Western Rivers) are similar to the LATERAL system described above but are numbered differently and use an additional daymark that is diamond shaped. This diamond shape means that the river channel crosses over to the other side as the daymark is approached. The numbers on the aids do not have lateral significance but, rather, indicate mileage from a fixed point (normally the river mouth.) Buoys are placed to mark the channel and are normally unmarked.

SUMMARY

AIDS TO NAVIGATION

This chapter explained buoy systems. Two types of systems: Uniform State Waterways Marking System (USWMS), and the LATERAL system were identified. The USWMS buoys are white with international orange markings. They alert us to danger, speed limit and piloting information. The LATERAL system buoys are defined by shapes and colors that have various meanings. The CAN buoy is green, ODD numbered, and marks the port side of the channel. NUN buoys are red, EVEN numbered, and mark the right side of the channel.

Buoys are in place for two reasons: to help the skipper navigate the waterways safely and to guide the skipper in the proper direction.

WHAT YOU WILL LEARN:

Use of Compass

Reading Nautical Charts

Reading Charts

CHAPTER 8

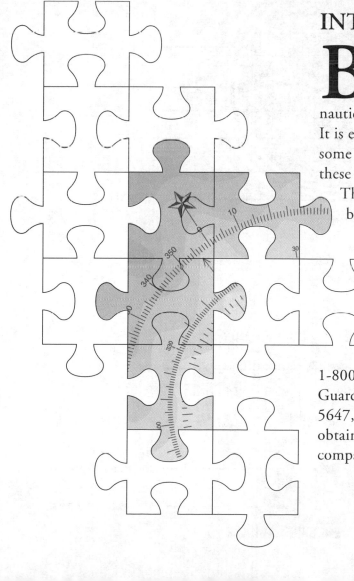

INTRODUCTION

Basic navigation for the recreational boater can be achieved with the help of an up-to-date nautical chart and a marine compass. It is essential for the skipper to have some knowledge and understanding of these two important boating aids.

This lesson will introduce the basics of navigation and chart reading. More information about courses on chart reading and compasses can be obtained by calling the Boat/US Course Line 1-800-336-2628 (in Virginia, 1-800-245-2628). The U.S. Coast Guard Customer Infoline, 1-800-368-5647, can also assist the skipper in obtaining information pertaining to compass and chart reading.

COMPASS

COMPASS:
Navigation
instrument, either
magnetic (showing
Magnetic North) or
gyro (showing True
North).

COMPASS CARD:
Part of a compass,
the card is
graduated in
degrees, to conform
with the magnetic,
meridian-referenced
direction system
inscribed with
direction which
remains constant;
the vessel turns, not
the card.

COMPASS ROSE:
The resulting figure
when the complete
360° directional
system is developed
as a circle with each
degree graduated
upon it, and with
the 000° indicated
as true north. Also
called true rose.
This is printed on
nautical charts for
determining
direction.

A **compass** can assist the skipper in getting to his destination. Basically, a compass has a fixed orientation — North to South. It also has a reference mark on the glass bubble, called a lubber's line. The numbers in degrees or letters (N, NW, W, etc.) on the floating **compass card** remain stationary, while the lubber's line actually turns with the boat. Keep electronic equipment and large ferrous metal objects away from the compass, since they can cause the compass to "deviate" from Magnetic North. It will be necessary to adjust the compass and calculate the deviation in order to determine the magnetic course. **Additional training beyond this course will be necessary to properly calculate this deviation.** Being able to steer a boat by the compass is particularly useful if land is out of sight, visibility is reduced, or the boater is disoriented.

The skipper, the boat, the passengers, as well as other boaters may depend on the boat's compass and the skipper's ability to use it properly. A compass card is designed to point to the Magnetic North Pole, which is slightly different than True North, depending on the exact location in the U.S. This is known as "variation." Each chart has a **compass rose** which shows the "variation" for that area.

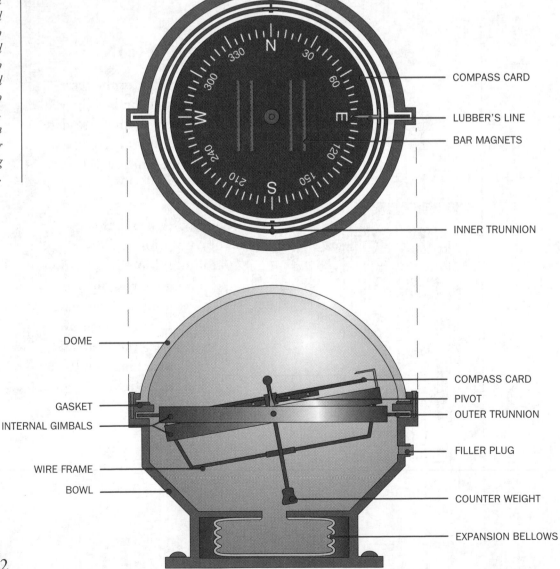

COMPASS CARD

LUBBER'S LINE

BAR MAGNETS

INNER TRUNNION

DOME

COMPASS CARD

PIVOT

OUTER TRUNNION

GASKET

INTERNAL GIMBALS

FILLER PLUG

WIRE FRAME

BOWL

COUNTER WEIGHT

EXPANSION BELLOWS

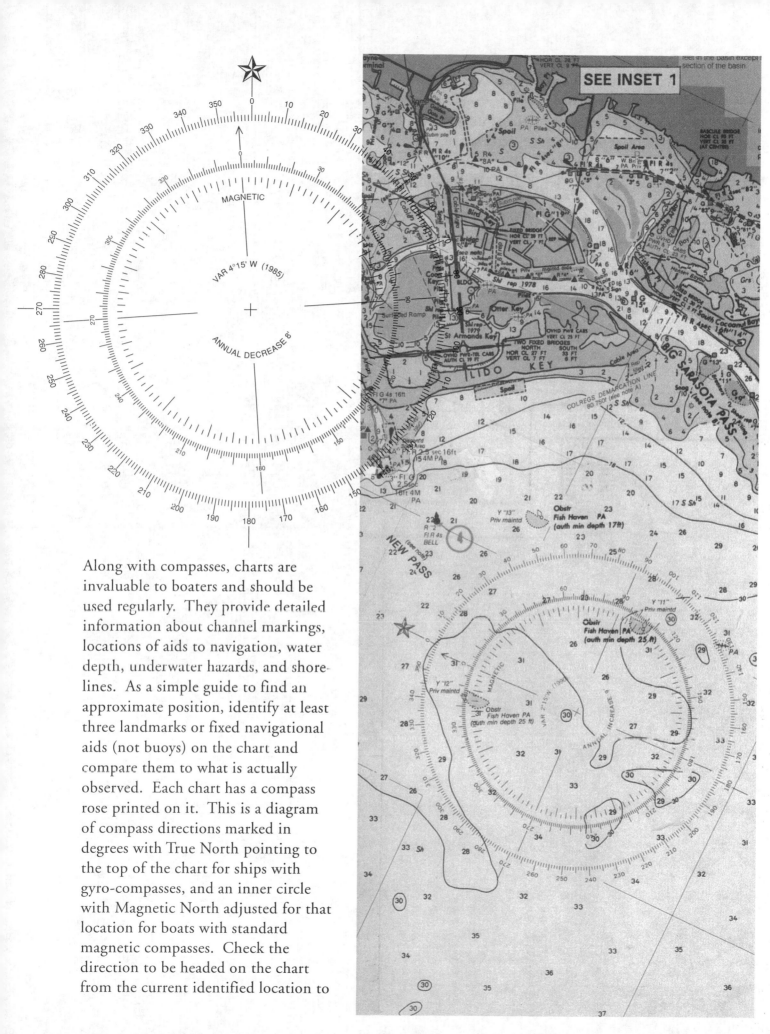

Along with compasses, charts are invaluable to boaters and should be used regularly. They provide detailed information about channel markings, locations of aids to navigation, water depth, underwater hazards, and shorelines. As a simple guide to find an approximate position, identify at least three landmarks or fixed navigational aids (not buoys) on the chart and compare them to what is actually observed. Each chart has a compass rose printed on it. This is a diagram of compass directions marked in degrees with True North pointing to the top of the chart for ships with gyro-compasses, and an inner circle with Magnetic North adjusted for that location for boats with standard magnetic compasses. Check the direction to be headed on the chart from the current identified location to the desired destination. Then steer the same direction in degrees on the boat compass as was plotted on the chart's magnetic compass rose and proceed to the destination.

SUMMARY

BASIC NAVIGATION AND CHART READING

This chapter taught the importance of compasses and charts.

Compass:

- Assists in getting the skipper to a destination.
- True north and Magnetic North are slightly different.

Charts:

Provide detailed information about channel markings, Aids to Navigation, and underwater hazards.

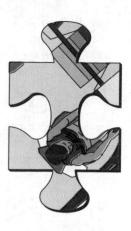

Maneuvering & Handling

CHAPTER 9

INTRODUCTION

Handling a boat is a skill that takes practice and experience. All boats handle differently. Even boats of the same design will handle differently. While there is no substitute for experience, the following information provides the information necessary to understand why a boat maneuvers as it does.

The console of many boats looks like a car. The challenge is that the boat does not have brakes, and it steers from the rear, not the front. In addition, the "road" moves, changing with the wind, tide and current.

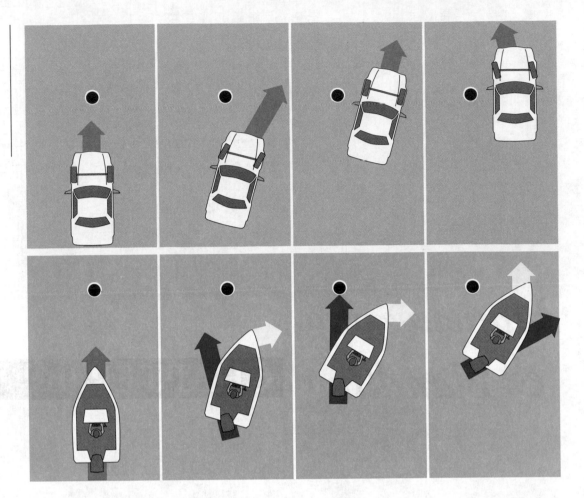

*RUDDER: A
vertical plate or
board for steering a
boat.*

*TILLER: A bar or
handle for turning a
boat's rudder or an
outboard motor.*

BOAT HANDLING

Steering

Boats turn by either using a **rudder** or by changing the direction of the propeller. Boats steer from the rear. Understanding this is critical while maneuvering next to a pier, another boat, or some other obstruction. If the skipper applies too

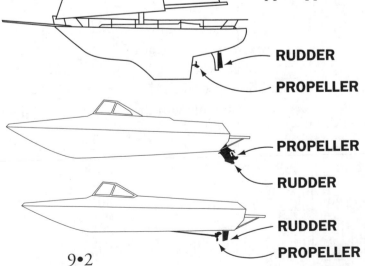

RUDDER

PROPELLER

PROPELLER

RUDDER

RUDDER

PROPELLER

much rudder before clearing the obstruction, the stern of the boat will collide with it.

Rudder

The rudder controls the direction of the boat. It is a vertical blade attached to a stock, normally at the stern behind the propeller; it is then attached to the steering wheel or tiller. By turning the wheel or swinging the **tiller**, water is deflected off the blade controlling the direction of the boat. The boat must be moving ahead or astern for the rudder to have any effect.

Propeller

Most boats are driven by one or more propellers that move in a circular motion. The pitch of the propeller produces water flow which spirals like the threads of a screw. When viewed from the stern, the propeller on most single-propeller boats turns in a clockwise direction and is referred to as "right-handed." In a dual-propeller configuration, the starboard screw is "right-handed."

THROTTLE IN REVERSE

It is important to know which type of propeller is on a boat because the rotation affects maneuverability, especially when backing. For instance, when in reverse, a "right-handed" propeller forces water against the starboard side of the hull pushing the stern to port requiring a considerable amount of right rudder and an increase in speed to compensate. On outboards and inboard/outboards, the rudder and propeller are located in one assembly that turns together. This makes them more maneuverable, but the stern of the boat will still have a tendency to "walk" in the direction that the propeller rotates while reversing.

Wind and Current

The design characteristics of a boat will dictate the effect that wind and current has on its maneuverability. The wind will have a greater effect on a boat with a shallow draft and high topside area. Conversely, a boat with a deep draft and low freeboard will be more affected by the current. Most powerboats have more of an exposed area and less weight at the bow than the stern, which results in the bow blowing downwind faster than the stern.

Practice will enable the skipper to develop the confidence necessary to maneuver skillfully. Throw a floating object overboard when in open water and practice maneuvering around it. Observe the length of time it takes for the boat to stop at various speeds, its turning radius and the effects of wind and current on its handling. Have other persons on the boat practice these maneuvers. If the skipper should fall overboard or become incapacitated, someone should be able to operate the boat.

REVIEW EXERCISE:

BOAT HANDLING

1. The rudder controls the _____ of the boat.

2. Boats steer from the _____.

CASTING OFF

Prior to casting off the mooring lines, conduct a safety check of the boat and surrounding area including the direction and force of wind and current. Test the engine(s) and gears.

Wind/Current off the Dock

Cast off all the lines and let the wind or current carry the boat clear. Be aware the boat may "spin" while drifting clear due to physical characteristics of the boat; e.g. freeboard and superstructure vs. center of mass.

Wind/Current onto the Dock

Leave the **bow spring line** (one of the standard dock lines, used to control fore and aft motion of a boat made fast to a pier or float) secured to the pier. Place a fender on the dockside bow. Turn the bow towards the dock and go ahead slowly to put tension on the spring line. When the stern is clear, throttle back and remove the line, shift the rudder (turn in opposite direction) and back down until the bow is clear of the dock. This method can be used when hemmed in between other boats and there is limited maneuvering room.

Turning in a Narrow Channel

In a single-propeller (right-handed) boat start the turn as close as possible to the port side of the channel. Put the rudder hard over to the right and alternate going forward and reverse until the bow points in the desired direction. Outboards, inboard/outboards and twin prop boats are able to turn easily in small areas.

ANCHORING

It is important to choose the correct anchor for the size of the boat and for the type of bottom in which the boat will be anchored. Ask experienced boaters or an established marine dealer to help decide which anchor will be best. Shown on page 9-5 are sketches of some different anchors.

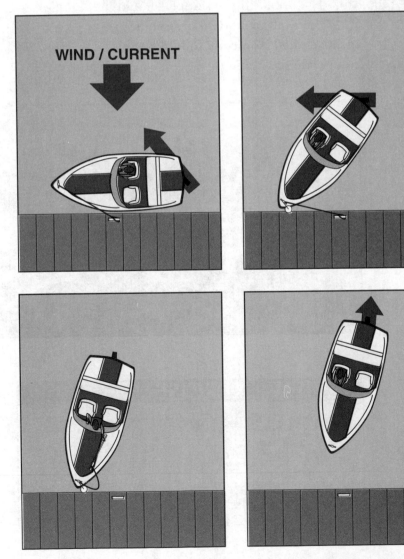

WIND / CURRENT

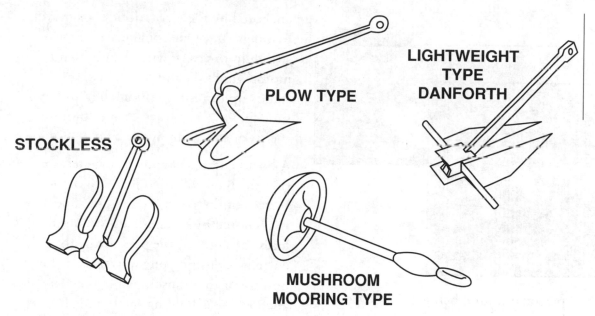

STOCKLESS

PLOW TYPE

LIGHTWEIGHT TYPE DANFORTH

MUSHROOM MOORING TYPE

The **ground tackle** assembly consists of the anchor, a short length of chain, various shackles or connectors, and the anchor line. Shown below is an illustration of ground tackle ready for use. Use of an anchor chain makes the setting of the anchor easier, eliminates chafing of the anchor line on the sea bed, and increases the holding power of the anchor.

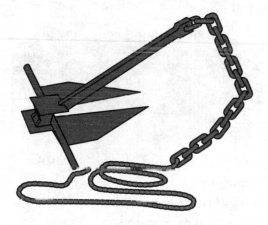

Coming Up To Anchor

Use some care in selecting the spot to anchor. Boats already anchored "own" that spot and can't be expected to move, so pick a spot that is well clear (even after paying out the anchor line). Be certain to leave plenty of room so the boat can swing, as well as allowing room for the other boats to swing. Skippers must keep in mind

the amount of line they and the other boats have out. If available, use buoys as reference points or, if close to shore, use a prominent land feature. Slow down to a speed where you're making minimum headway, keeping the bow into the wind and/or current. Head in such a way that the effects of both water current and wind are neutralized. On approaching the anchoring point, bring the engine to neutral and drift into position. When the boat is

"dead" in the water, let the engine idle in neutral. Lower, <u>do not throw</u>, the anchor over the side. Throwing the anchor often causes it to foul with the rode (anchor line), and can lead to

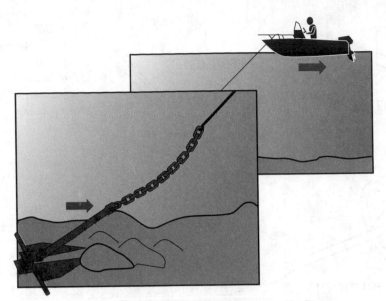

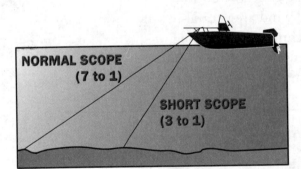

NORMAL SCOPE (7 to 1)

SHORT SCOPE (3 to 1)

personal injury, being pulled overboard, or even incurring damage to the boat.

After the anchor is on the bottom, pay out the anchor line gradually as the boat drifts back from the anchor point due to wind and/or current. As a general rule, pay out five to ten times as much anchor line as the depth of the water. If the wind or current is fairly strong, increase the amount of line paid out (called the **scope**). The line should be properly secured to the boat.

Take a couple of turns of the anchor line around the anchor bitt or cleat and secure with a figure eight. Above all, keep feet and legs well clear of the anchor line. Many people have been injured by the tremendous forces that can be generated in anchor lines.

Anchor By The Bow

Always anchor by the bow. Every year many boats capsize and several people die because they anchored by the sterns. The accident scenarios are distressingly similar. An angler,

anchored by the stern, decides to move to a new spot. He is in a small boat, sitting in the stern with the outboard motor, gas tank, and tackle box. He stands up to retrieve the anchor and suddenly a "freak wave" comes over the stern and swamps the boat.

A boat is designed and constructed so that the bow will rise up and over the surface of the water. The stern is not. If anchored by the stern, as the stern faces the current, the pressure of the current is pushing one way against the bottom of the transom while the anchor line is holding the top of the same transom against the current. This lever action greatly increases the tension on the anchor line, which in

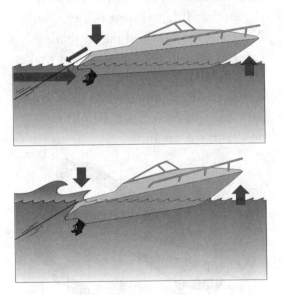

turn pulls the stern deeper into, and sometimes under, the water. Therefore, anchoring should always be from the bow, which is designed to rise up and over the water regardless of the speed of the current.

Retrieving the Anchor

When retrieving the anchor (weighing anchor), proceed slowly until the boat is directly over the anchor. Retrieve the line as it becomes available. If the anchor does not break free easily,

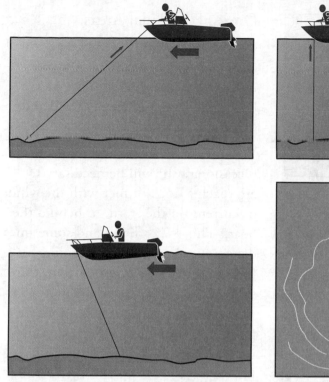

SCOPE: The ratio of line paid out to the depth of the water.

TRIP LINE: A line fast to the crown of the anchor by means of which it can be hauled on out when dug too deeply or fouled; a similar line used on a sea anchor to bring it aboard.

secure the line to the cleat and go ahead slowly. If it still does not break free, let out a little line and run the boat in circles keeping the line taut.

Use of a **trip line** is the best way to break out a fouled anchor. Use a light line, but one strong enough to stand the pull of a snagged anchor (3/8 inch polypropylene — which floats — is a typical choice). Attach this line to the crown of the anchor. The trip line should be just long enough to reach the surface of the water. Pass the line through a wooden or foam float (a plastic bottle with a handle can be used) and end the line in a small eye splice that can be brought up with a boat hook. If the anchor doesn't trip

in a normal manner, pick up the "trip" line and haul the anchor up crown first.

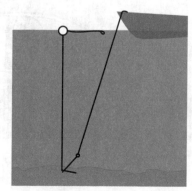

REVIEW EXERCISE: ANCHORING

1. When anchoring the boat, lower the anchor from the _____.

2. When approaching the anchoring point, bring the engine to _____and _____into position.

3. When anchoring, take a couple of turns around the anchor bitt or cleat and tie a_____ knot.

9•7

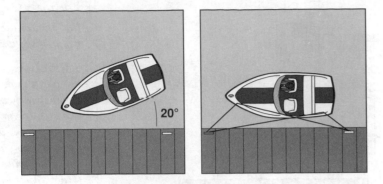

DOCKING

The waters near a dock or pier should always be treated with the same respect and caution as a parking lot that might be slippery — where a sudden turn or change of speed could cause the driver to lose control.

Approach the dock or pier slowly, with alternating stop/slow-advance/stop/slow-advance actions. If possible, approach the dock or pier into the wind and current.

NOTE: Wind and current may not be in the same direction. Select the strongest force, and drive against it. This way there is power and control. Remember: A slow approach is seldom a bad approach!

Twenty degrees is typically a good approach angle. It's about the same angle used to approach a curb with a car when parallel parking. Tie up the bow first and then the stern.

Docking In Tidal Areas

On the approach, if the wind and/or current are moving toward the pier, make the move parallel to the pier, a bit farther out, and let the wind and/or current push the boat toward the docking space.

Occasionally, it will be necessary to approach a dock or pier with the wind or current on the stern, or behind the boat. This is a difficult and sometimes dangerous maneuver. Depending on the speed of the wind or current, the skipper may have to put the motor in slow reverse to approach the dock or pier. Approach at a slight angle this time and gently swing parallel; but HAVE THE STERN LINE READY — and tie it to the dock first this time. Waves may splash over the stern, if the stern is into the waves, especially in small boats.

Docking is really a maneuver that takes practice, much as it took practice (and no substitute for it) to learn how to back a car into a parallel parking spot.

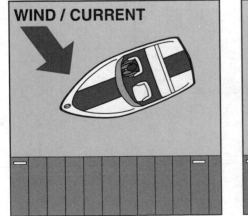

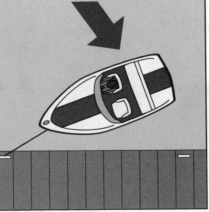

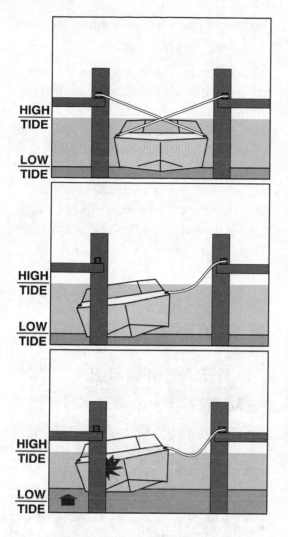

Securing The Boat In A Tidal Area

When securing the boat in a tidal area, the spring lines should be placed at about a 45-degree angle to the boat. That will leave enough line for the boat to safely rise or fall with the tide. Questions to consider when docking in a tidal area are: What is the speed and force of the current? What can damage the boat? Will the boat go under the pier at low tide and be crushed at high tide?

Mooring The Boat

Tying a boat to a pier or mooring requires more than just a good knot; it also requires some preliminary thought. Some considerations are how close are other boats and how much does the water rise and fall?

FOUL-WEATHER HANDLING

Being caught in bad weather in a small boat can be a frightening experience for the new boater. Always "keep an eye on the weather." Some types of bad weather cannot be predicted with great accuracy — line squalls (a sudden violent wind often accompanied by rain), thunderstorms, local fogs and the like. When wind and water start to build, it's time to head for shelter. It is also time to be certain everyone is wearing their PFD and it is securely fastened. If there is heavy wave action, steer the boat so that the bow takes the waves slightly on one side or the other. Be careful to use only enough power to keep the boat heading into the waves — do not let it pound. A little pitching and tossing is a lot safer than rolling. If the boat has a relatively high freeboard at the stern, it might be safe to lift the stern to the waves and head into shelter. If shelter is not close by, or safe to proceed to, then stay "put" and ride out the bad weather.

Outboards with a low transom should never be run in a **following sea** because the waves are often traveling at high speeds and can wash into the boat over the stern, swamping the boat and drowning the engine.

There are certain waters that are best to avoid if at all possible. Examples of these are: Areas where river currents meet ocean currents or other river currents; Areas immediately above and below dams; Inlets and harbor entrances where the entrance is narrow and there is shallow water over shoals (navigational hazard). These can get the unwary skipper into serious trouble.

REVIEW EXERCISE:

FOUL-WEATHER HANDLING

1. If out on a boat and the weather begins to deteriorate, the first thing to do is to _____ _____.

2. When heading into heavy waves it is generally best to steer the boat so that the bow takes the waves _____.

3. Outboards with a low transom should never be run in a _____ sea.

Knots

Knowing how to tie a variety of knots is a good idea for boat operators. Study the examples on the following page.

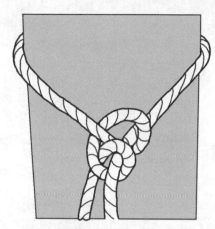

Two half hitch: The knot is tied by first passing the end around the object and under the standing part. The end is then passed around the standing part and under itself. This is the first half hitch. The second hitch is formed the same way.

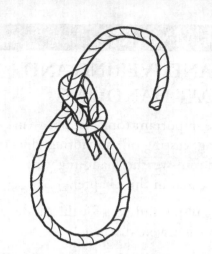

Bowline: Form a loop in the standing part with the end side of the loop on top. The end is then passed up through the loop, around behind the standing part and back down through the loop.

Anchor Bend: The knot is begun by passing the end around the object twice. The end is then passed around the standing part and through the two loops previously made around the object. The end is again passed by the same side of the standing part in the same direction, around the standing part and between the standing part and itself.

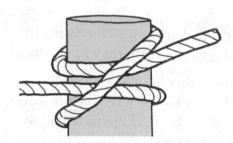

Clove Hitch: It is tied by looping the end of the line around the object twice in the same direction, once below, and once above, the standing part.

Double Becket Bend: It is tied by forming a bight in the bigger line and passing the smaller line's end up from under the bight, then passing the smaller line around behind the bigger line, and back under itself twice.

Belay to a Cleat: The best method is to lead the line in one round turn around the base of the cleat and then form at least one figure eight around the horns of the cleat. Secure with a half hitch around one horn of the cleat.

9•11

SUMMARY

MANEUVERING AND BOAT HANDLING

The important topics of boat handling, casting off, anchoring, docking and foul-weather handling were discussed in this chapter.

The terms and uses for the rudder and propeller were discussed.

Unlike cars, boats steer from the rear. This is important to remember when casting off and docking.

Anchoring: Choosing the right anchor for a boat is important.

Anchor by the bow.

Docking: Slowly is the operative word.

Be aware that the water is constantly changing, so be careful when docking.

Foul-weather handling: Steer so that the boat takes the wave slightly on one side of the bow. If shelter is not near, ride out the bad weather.

Emergency Procedures

CHAPTER 10

INTRODUCTION

Recreational boating is an enjoyable sport. Knowing and using safe boating practices can minimize the danger of accidents while afloat. This chapter will outline what a responsible skipper should do in an emergency. **Remember, severe conditions may dictate other procedures.** The information presented in this section applies as a general rule.

Practicing emergency procedures in a safe, controlled environment will assist the skipper in dealing with real emergencies in a proficient and safe manner.

This section of the book will cover several "common emergencies" such as: falls overboard, capsizing and swamping, fire, running aground, medical emergencies, and mechanical and fuel problems.

FALLS OVERBOARD

A serious contributor to fatal boating accidents is falling overboard. Although the leading cause of falls overboard is unknown, it is believed that many of these accidents are related to standing/leaning over the edge of the boat (**gunwale**).

Standing or leaning over the gunwale for whatever reason can easily lead to a person being pitched off balance by wakes, waves, or movement of another passenger, especially on small lightweight boats. But, falls overboard occur with surprising frequency from large boats, as well. Skippers and passengers must all be informed of, and alert to the potential danger of falling overboard. Do not permit passengers to sit on the gunwale, or to let their arms or legs hang over the side or the bow. Anytime people move about in the boat, they should be aware of any waves or wakes which may cause the boat to pitch or roll suddenly. There is an old seafaring rule that applies here— "One hand for the ship — one hand for yourself" — meaning "hang on"! Tight turns without warning passengers, slipping on wet surfaces, or just plain horseplay can all result in falls overboard. A good rule to follow is to maintain three points of contact with the boat - either two feet and one hand or two hands and one foot, while moving about.

Overboard Drill

Recovering a person who has fallen overboard is an important procedure to practice. Also, all members of the crew should be well rehearsed in these procedures in case the skipper should fall overboard. As a review, a few simple precautions can prevent falls overboard:

1. Avoid alcohol consumption.

2. Avoid sitting on decks, gunwales, or seat backs.

3. Use handholds when standing or moving within the boat; maintain three points of contact.

4. Warn passengers of all maneuvers, especially turns and speed changes.

5. Be careful of footing; watch for slippery or uneven surfaces. Use appropriate footwear.

6. Avoid "horseplay."

Wear your PFD! This lessens the risk to life considerably should you find yourself overboard.

RESCUE

There are two forms of rescue in an overboard situation. They are based upon the person's swimming ability, the ability to self-rescue, and to a lesser extent, on the weather and water conditions.

Self-Rescue

The simplest technique is self-rescue. This is possible under limited circumstances when the uninjured person can swim back to the boat. The boat operator needs only to stop the boat and throw a flotation device to the person in the water (if the person is not wearing one) before turning the boat; then have the person swim to the boat. A "PFD" is best, but don't delay while hunting for one. An empty gas tank, a styrofoam ice cooler, a spare oar or paddle, etc. all float and will help keep the person afloat until a PFD can be thrown. Maintain a constant watch on the person in the water while returning for the pickup. If possible, have another person onboard serve as a spotter. The spotter's job is to keep the person in

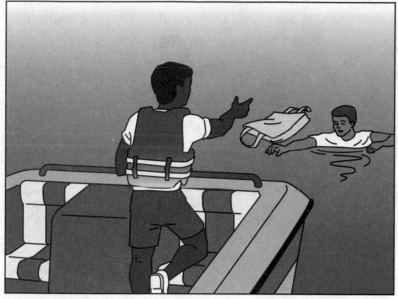

"Keep an eye on the person in the water until he/she is aboard safely."

accidentally knocking it into gear during the confusion of helping the person aboard.

Assisted Rescue

If a person is hurt or unconscious, or for some reason cannot swim to the boat, a different rescue method is used. If the person in the water is able to grasp and hold a line, maneuver the boat upwind close to them and then turn off the engine. Then throw the person in the water a line and pull them alongside. If the person in the water is unable to grasp and hold a line, maneuver the boat windward or to the "weather side," turn off the engine and let the boat drift down to the person in the water. As the boat drifts alongside, take any action necessary to retrieve the person without aggravating or causing further injury. Always keep the operator's side of the boat alongside the person in the water. NEVER RETRIEVE ANYONE FROM THE WATER WITH THE ENGINE RUNNING! The propeller of an idling engine may still turn fast enough to cause injury even when the gear shift is in neutral.

WINDWARD:
Toward the direction from which the wind is coming

the water in sight and to point to them the whole time. This enables the skipper to concentrate on operating the boat safely and helps to insure the safety of the person in the water.

Approach the person as if approaching a mooring buoy. Proceed at a slow speed and make the final approach slightly to **windward**. Shut off the motor when within reaching distance of the person in the water. Even though the gearshift is in neutral, the propeller can spin fast enough to cause severe injury. Also, if the motor is left running, there is always the danger of

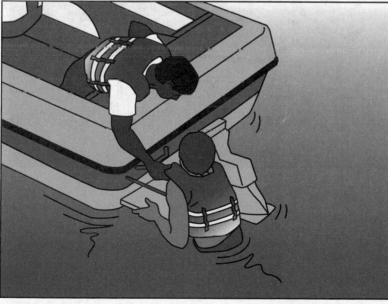

"Bringing a person aboard — a boarding ladder may be necessary."

10•3

A general rule is to turn the bow of the boat into the wind, whether under power or in a sailboat. Maneuvering a boat alongside a person in the water is one of the most difficult and demanding tasks a boat operator has to perform. It requires a lot of practice.

CAPSIZED

Only as a last resort should anyone go into the water, and only then if the person has on a PFD (no matter how good a swimmer they claim to be). Remember this rule: NEVER GO IN THE WATER UNLESS APPROPRIATELY EQUIPPED AND TRAINED. Possibly the single most difficult problem will be the transfer of the person from the water into the boat. In general, the person in the boat should make contact with the person in the water, and when practical, bring them towards the stern of the boat. Then, while facing the person in the water, grab the person underneath the shoulders of the PFD and hoist. It may take several attempts to get the person into the boat. The person should get his or her chest over the transom and swing a leg into the boat. Practice this procedure.

CAPSIZING AND SWAMPING

Capsizing is the overturning of a boat to an upside-down position.

Swamping is filling a boat with water, but remaining afloat and usually upright.

SWAMPED

Capsizing almost always results in a swamped boat, but swamping rarely involves capsizing. In either case there will be a boat full of water floating at the surface with its passengers in the water.

Always remain with the boat unless there is danger of it being carried into more dangerous areas, such as waterfalls, dams, breaking surf, or intakes for a hydro-electric plant.

If the boat capsizes in cold water, get as far out of the water as possible. To prevent hypothermia (an effect of cold water on the body), keep as much clothing on as possible. Bright colors will assist rescuers in visually locating you in the water. Keep all people together; do not separate. STAY WITH THE BOAT.

Most small boats continue to float even when turned over or full of water. Take care of yourself first, then the passengers. Do not worry about gear drifting off. Enter the boat from over the sides and from opposite sides if there is more than one of you. Enter the boat near **amidships**. Reach over the gunwale and place both hands on the bottom; then kick your feet to the surface and slide over the gunwale. Push down on the gunwale as little as possible, otherwise the boat may roll and turn over. When your hips clear the gunwale, roll over to a face up position and sit on the bottom with your lower legs sticking out over the side. Make sure the boat is stable; then swing your legs aboard. Stay seated in the bottom of the boat and keep your weight low. Small boats can be paddled to shore using oars, paddles or hands. If there is buoyancy and the boat is small and the gunwales are above water, the boat can be bailed.

Finally, be ready to give a distress signal— but save the signals until it's evident that there's a good chance somebody will see them.

FIRE AFLOAT

A fire while afloat is a very harrowing experience. Fire safety is something that everyone who owns or operates a boat should practice. Choices are limited when fire occurs on the water. When the source of the fire stems from materials such as wood or fabric (e.g. mattress or rags), put it out with water, using the bailing bucket. If the fire is in loose materials, it may be best to simply heave them over the side into the water. If the fire is oil, grease, or some kind of fuel, use the fire extinguisher, but be aware of reflash. Point the nozzle at the base of the flames. Remember, a fire must have fuel, air, and heat to continue burning. Take away any one of the three and it will go out. Because air enters a fire at the base of the fire, always aim the nozzle of the extinguisher toward the base.

If the boat is underway and a fire starts, stop the boat. A moving boat adds air to the fire, causing a hotter and more dangerous fire. Be certain to place and keep people upwind of fire and smoke. Anchor, if appropriate, to hold the boat in a position so that the fire remains downwind. In this way, it is less likely to spread to the rest of the boat. Close all hatches and radio for assistance, if possible. Turn off electrical power.

If forced to abandon the boat because of fire or explosion, get everyone into PFDs, stay together, and get clear of the boat. Use any available floating debris to keep afloat.

AGROUND

When boating in shallow lakes, streams, tidal waters, or in any area where the water level is subject to change, there's a chance of running **aground**. As in all emergency situations, the first thing to do is to stay calm. Usually, the first impulse is to shift immediately into reverse, gun the engine, and attempt to back up. This could be the wrong move. If aground on sand or mud, the propeller spinning in reverse might pull more sand and mud under the keel, making matters worse. However, a little sand and mud is nothing compared with possible damage to the propeller, outdrive, shaft, and engine, as well as to the hull. Therefore, it is best to stay calm and assess the situation prior to taking action to clear the boat from the grounding site.

If the boat is aground:

1. Look to see if the current or the wind is working with or against the boat. Get a sample of the bottom.

2. Test the depths around the boat with a paddle or boat hook to see where the water is deepest.

3. Look for leaks.

There are many options for removing a boat which has run aground. Here are a few:

1. Push off with a boat hook or paddle.

2. Shift the weight around in the boat to either keep the boat from going aground further (make it heavy at the point of contact) or to allow the bow of the boat to lift up farther (make it light at the point of contact).

3. If in a sailboat, a winch can possibly pull the bow of the boat from a grounding situation. A line should run from the **kedge** (anchor) (set at 45-degrees to the wind or current), to the bow of the boat and onto the winch. This may pull the bow free.

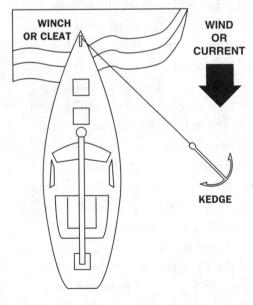

4. If the bottom is shallow and sandy, and it is safe to do so, get a couple of people into PFDs and out of the boat to push it off. REMEMBER, do not endanger the individuals in the water by extended exposure to cold water (hypothermia) or fast

currents. Additionally, consideration must be given for providing a safe re-entry into the boat.

5. If conditions will allow, get an anchor in the deeper water and pull the bow around. Don't let the wind push the boat sideways into the shallow water.

Having the passengers move and shift their weight may get results. However, if the boat has run up on a rock or something solid, check to see if there is damage to the hull, through hull fittings, etc., before trying to back off. It might be wiser to keep the boat on the rock until something can be stuffed into the hole. A PFD, mattress, or blanket jammed into the hole may help long enough to get to shore. Waterproof tape and wooden plugs may also help. If the hole is too big, get all passengers into PFDs and stay with the boat. Most boats will not sink immediately, if at all. There's extra flotation in most boats — just hang on until help arrives.

MECHANICALLY DISABLED

Usually when a boat is disabled, it is due to some sort of trouble with the power (engine/sails) or steering systems. For most engines there are three "soft" spots where trouble is likely to occur: the drive train (propeller, shear pin, etc.), the electrical and ignition system, and the fuel system.

If the propeller strikes the bottom or a rock, breaking the shear pin (the shear pin is designed to break, which prevents serious damage to the engine), or spinning the rubber hub, the engine races with no forward motion of the

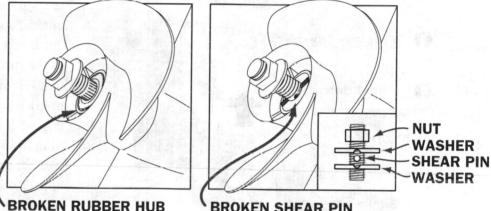

BROKEN RUBBER HUB   **BROKEN SHEAR PIN**

NUT
WASHER
SHEAR PIN
WASHER

REVIEW EXERCISE:

AGROUND

1. If the boat runs aground, test the depth with a _____ or _____.

2. It is often possible to push off by having the passengers _____ _____.

3. Never get out of the boat to push off without first _____ the bottom and putting on a _____.

boat. When this happens, shut off the engine and pocket the ignition key. Anchor the boat to avoid drifting into shallow water. Get out the tool box, which should contain spare shear pins, cotter keys and a pair of pliers. If the hub has spun, the propeller will have to be replaced. Make sure the engine is in neutral gear, release the reversing locking lever, and raise and lock the engine so that the propeller is out of the water. *(See diagram on page 10-8)*

Install and bend the new cotter pin to avoid loss. Wise skippers carry at least two spare cotter pins and a spare propeller, since propeller blades do break off occasionally. Carry two pairs of pliers, two common sized wrenches, and at least two sets of standard and phillips screw drivers at all times. The use of a lanyard taped to the tool helps prevent loss. If any one is lost, there will be a spare and often two pairs of pliers can come in handy!

Electrical System

When the engine won't start, or it quits suddenly, the first and easiest thing to check is the fuel level and fuel line. If there is adequate fuel and the fuel line is not clogged, check the spark plugs. From the boat box, get out the spare plugs and plug wrench (an inexpensive and handy tool). Make sure the engine gears are in neutral and ignition key (if one is used) is in your pocket. Remove the engine cover. Carefully detach the plug leads and remove the plugs. Inspect the plug electrodes. If they appear oily or black with carbon, replace them with spare plugs. If spare plugs are not available, try cleaning the electrode and re-gapping the plug. If the plug is ok, check to see that the metal plug gasket is in place, and put the plug back in. Look for corroded, dirty, damaged, or loose connections. Check for broken or damaged spark plug wires. Also,

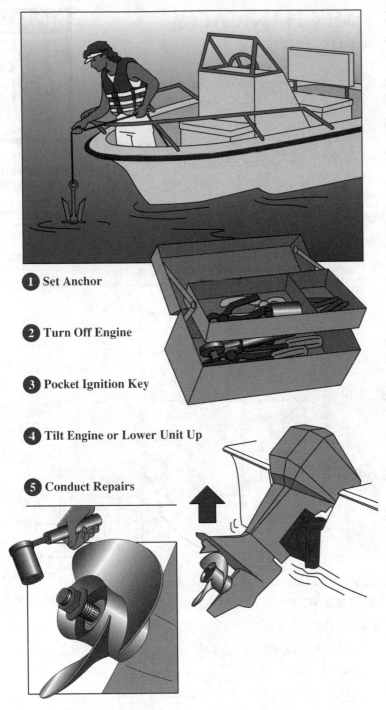

1. **Set Anchor**

2. **Turn Off Engine**

3. **Pocket Ignition Key**

4. **Tilt Engine or Lower Unit Up**

5. **Conduct Repairs**

With a pair of pliers, straighten and remove the propeller hub cotter pin. It may be necessary to slide the propeller from the drive shaft to remove the broken shear pin. Replace the propeller on the drive shaft and line up the shear pin holes in the propeller and drive shaft. Be careful not to drop the new pin in the water (a good reason to carry multiple spare parts). Insert the new shear pin. Replace the propeller hub on the drive shaft.

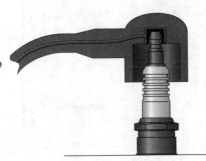

Clean Spark Plug   **Fouled Spark Plug**

and bowl. Disconnect the coil wire from the distributor. Remove the fuel line from the outlet side of the fuel pump and crank the engine. If no fuel comes out of the pump, the pump is the trouble. If fuel is present, reconnect the fuel lines to the carburetor and remove the spark plugs.

CAUTION: Do not allow gasoline to spill into the boat. If the plugs are dry (no fuel on them), the trouble is in the carburetor. Check the inlet filter, the choke, and the adjustment of the main jet.

If the plugs are wet, the engine may be flooded. Open the throttle wide, put the choke in the full-open position, and with the ignition on, crank over the engine. This draws only air through the engine and will quickly dry it out.

check the wiring between the coil and the distributor cap. Dry any wet wiring or connections. If the engine is overheated, it may not start until it has cooled.

WARNING: Disconnect battery leads prior to working on the electrical system. Before attempting any electrical repairs, make sure bilges and engine compartments are free of explosive vapors.

Fuel Problems

Check the tank. If there is plenty of fuel in the tank, check lines and filters on the fuel pump and carburetor. If no gas is in the bowl, the trouble may be a clogged or poorly connected fuel line. Make sure the fuel tank vent is open. Remove the sediment bowl, clean the filter and replace the filter

REVIEW EXERCISE:

MECHANICALLY DISABLED AND FUEL PROBLEMS

1. Trouble is most likely to occur in a gasoline engine in one of three systems. These systems are:

   a. _____

   b. _____

   c. _____

2. The shear pin is designed to break and prevent _____.

DISTRESS SIGNALS (MANAGING YOUR OWN RESCUE)

When an emergency occurs and help is required from another boat, the Coast Guard or the marine patrol may be contacted by radio or telephone. It is necessary to notify them of your location and direct them to the boat. Emergencies never seem to happen at convenient times. Often it's dark or the waves are high enough that visibility is difficult. Standard distress signals can help others arrive more quickly. How visible is the boat? It may appear as just a speck on the water. How can it be more visible during a rescue? Can it be seen by radar or is it all fiberglass or wood and not visible on a radar screen. (Special Radar Reflectors are sold, but in an emergency a roll of aluminum foil stretched vertically on boat hooks or paddles may be helpful). Display a distress flag and use Visual Distress Signals (VDS) and audible distress signals to attract attention.

Visual Distress Signals *(as discussed earlier)*

A. Arm Waving

B. SOS - Mirror

C. Distress Flag

D. Flares and Pyrotechnics

Pyrotechnic Visual Distress Signals (VDS) must be Coast Guard Approved, in serviceable condition, and readily accessible. They are marked with a date showing the service life, which must not be exceeded to be legally carried.

If pyrotechnic devices are selected to meet VDS carriage requirements, a minimum of three signals for day use

and three signals for night are required. Some pyrotechnic signals meet both day and night-use requirements.

These signals can be used to attract help and to direct help to the boat's location when rescuers arrive in the area.

Continuous use of the Morse Code SOS — three short blasts or flashes followed by three long and then three short — is a well-known international signal for distress.

Marine VHF Radio Distress Calls

Detailed radio rules and procedures can be obtained from various sources, such as the publication *Maritime Radio Users Handbook*.

The marine radio is the best device for calling for help. The distress, safety, and calling frequencies, (VHF-FM channel 16 (156.8 MHz) and medium frequency (MF)(2182 kHz) are continuously monitored by Coast Guard ships and search and rescue stations as well as by most other ships and commercial vessels.

Citizens Band (CB) radio is not monitored by Coast Guard stations or ships. However, some Coast Guard units have the capability to operate on CB radio channels and can respond if notified by other means that a boater

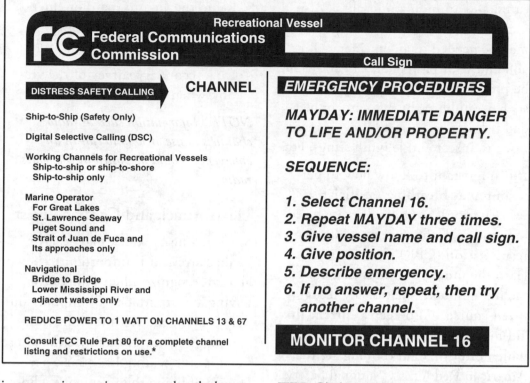

Recreational Vessel

Federal Communications Commission

Call Sign

DISTRESS SAFETY CALLING ➤	CHANNEL

Ship-to-Ship (Safety Only)

Digital Selective Calling (DSC)

Working Channels for Recreational Vessels
Ship-to-ship or ship-to-shore
Ship-to-ship only

Marine Operator
For Great Lakes
St. Lawrence Seaway
Puget Sound and
Strait of Juan de Fuca and
Its approaches only

Navigational
Bridge to Bridge
Lower Mississippi River and
adjacent waters only

REDUCE POWER TO 1 WATT ON CHANNELS 13 & 67

Consult FCC Rule Part 80 for a complete channel
listing and restrictions on use.*

EMERGENCY PROCEDURES

MAYDAY: IMMEDIATE DANGER TO LIFE AND/OR PROPERTY.

SEQUENCE:

1. Select Channel 16.
2. Repeat MAYDAY three times.
3. Give vessel name and call sign.
4. Give position.
5. Describe emergency.
6. If no answer, repeat, then try another channel.

MONITOR CHANNEL 16

is requesting assistance and only has a CB radio. CB cannot be considered an adequate substitute for a marine band radio for safety purposes.

Request assistance from the Coast Guard on the marine radio by calling "Coast Guard" on channel 16 or 2182 kHz, and describe the situation.

When you have a life or death emergency and require immediate assistance, you transmit the distress call, "Mayday–Mayday–Mayday–this is ...(Name of the vessel/call sign)...(The position)...(Describe emergency)... Over."

REVIEW EXERCISE:
DISTRESS

1. To request life or death emergency assistance on the radio, use the distress signal

_____

2. An easily recognized distress signal that does not require equipment is: (write answer in your own words).

_____

FIRST AID

Since there is no substitute for first aid training, first aid will not be elaborated on in this section. However, attention will be given to those situations which may arise while boating.

It is important to know first aid and to have a properly supplied first aid kit on board. Examine and review the contents of the first aid kit on a regular basis. The container for the first aid kit should be made of a waterproof material, such as plastic or soft nylon/vinyl; avoid metal, which could rust, or cardboard, which could soak up moisture.

Suggested items that should be included in the kit are: 1-inch and 2-inch gauze roller bandages; various size adhesive strips; 1-inch, 2-inch, and 4-inch gauze pads; several triangular bandages (minimum of 40 inches); several elastic bandages (various sizes); absorbent cotton; cotton-tipped applicators; waterproof adhesive tape; scissors; antiseptic liquids and ointment; aspirin and/or aspirin substi-

*See Preface

tutes, and ammonia inhalants. Also include personal medicine(s) which may be needed in an emergency for you and your passengers. In addition, be prepared to handle emergencies, such as sunburn, burns, cuts, imbedded fish hooks, splinters, severe reactions to insect and jellyfish stings, etc.

It is important to know how to perform rescue breathing (artificial resuscitation), to control severe bleeding, and to perform cardiopulmonary resuscitation (CPR) if necessary. To learn the most up-to-date first aid techniques, take a nationally recognized course. Also keep a current first aid manual on board. Organizations which offer first aid training are the American Red Cross, National Safety Council, etc. Those offering CPR are the American Heart Association, American Red Cross, National Safety Council, etc.

Emergency Action Principles

Developing first aid common sense is an important part of providing first aid care. First aid, properly given, can reduce the effects of injuries and medical emergencies, can keep a seriously ill or injured person alive, and can mean the difference between a short and long hospital stay. Proper first aid must be given quickly and effectively or the victim's condition may become more serious by the time further help arrives on the scene.

In the excitement of an emergency, it is important to stop for a moment to clear the mind and to think before acting. When responding to an emergency situation, remain calm and apply the **four emergency action principles:**

1. Survey the scene.
2. Do a primary survey of the victim.

3. Radio the Coast Guard or emergency medical services (EMS) system for help.

4. Do a secondary survey of the victim, when appropriate.

NOTE: Information such as radio channels to use or who to call in an emergency should be posted at the boat's radio.

Heart Attack and Cardiac Arrest

Since any heart attack may lead to cardiac arrest, it is important to be able to recognize when someone is having a heart attack. Prompt action may prevent the victim's heart from stopping. A heart attack victim whose heart is still beating has a far better chance of living than someone whose heart has stopped. Most people who die from a heart attack die within two hours after having the heart attack. Many of these people could have been saved if the person having the heart attack, and the bystanders, had been able to recognize the signals of a heart attack and had taken prompt action.

Signals of a Heart Attack

The most significant signal of a heart attack is chest discomfort or pain. A victim may describe it as uncomfortable pressure, squeezing, a fullness or tightness, aching, crushing, constricting, oppressive, or heavy. The pain may spread to one or both shoulders, to the arms or to the neck, jaw, or back (see figure at top of page 10-13).

In addition to chest pain, other signals may include:

- Sweating.
- Nausea.
- Shortness of breath.

Many victims deny that they are having a heart attack. They may not

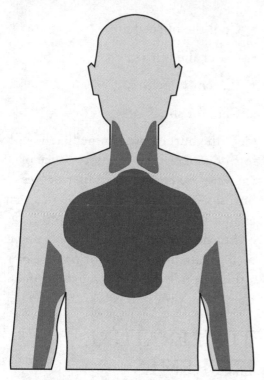

want to admit to themselves or to others that they are having a heart attack. This denial may delay medical care when it is needed most.

First Aid for a Heart Attack

To respond quickly in case of heart attack:

1. Recognize the signals of a heart attack and take action.

2. Have the victim stop what he or she is doing and sit or lie down in a comfortable position. Loosen restrictive clothing. Do not let the victim move around.

3. Have someone radio for help. If alone, make time for the call. A key factor in whether or not a victim will survive a heart attack is how quickly the victim receives advanced care. Therefore, it is important to call for medical help right away before the condition gets worse and the heart stops.

Because the heart attack victim's heart may stop beating (cardiac arrest), be prepared to give CPR. For additional information regarding CPR and other

first aid skills, contact the local office of the American Heart Association, American Red Cross, or National Safety Council for additional information.

Burns

Burns are injuries resulting from exposure to heat, chemicals, electricity, or radiation. The severity of a burn depends on the temperature of the object or material causing the burn, how long the skin was exposed to the source, the location and extent of the burn, and the victim's age and medical condition.

Types of Burns

Burns are classified according to the source — such as heat or chemicals — and the depth. The deeper the burn, the more severe it is. Generally, there are three depth classifications: first-degree (superficial); second-degree (partial thickness); and third-degree (full thickness).

First-degree burns involve only the top layer of skin. The skin is red and dry, and the burn is usually painful.

Second-degree burns are deeper than first-degree burns. The burned skin will look red and have blisters.

Third-degree burns extend through the skin and into the structures below the skin. These burns may look brown or charred (black). The tissues underneath may look white. (See diagram on page 10-14.)

First Aid for Heat Burns

If the scene is safe, do a primary survey. Call for advanced medical help if necessary. Look for burns on the face, especially around the nose or mouth. If there are burns on the face, continually monitor the victim's

BURNS

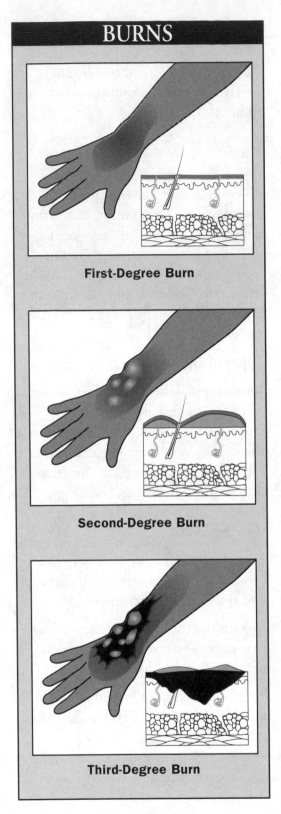

First-Degree Burn

Second-Degree Burn

Third-Degree Burn

breathing. These burns may signal that the airway or lungs are burned.

If burns are present, follow these four basic care steps:

- Cool the burned area.
- Cover the burned area.
- Prevent infection.
- Care for shock.

Cool the burned area immediately with lots of cool water. Do not use ice or ice water except on small first-degree burns. Apply wet cloths to an area that cannot be immersed. Do not put ointments on any burn that will receive medical attention. Do not try to clean a third-degree burn. To prevent infection, do not break blisters.

TEMPERATURE EXTREMES

Heat Emergencies

On hot, humid days with no breeze, anyone may be affected by the heat. People who are especially susceptible to extreme heat are the very young and the very old, the chronically ill, the overweight, those who work in hot places, and athletes. They may suffer heat stroke, heat exhaustion, or heat cramps.

Heat Stroke

Heat stroke is life-threatening. The victim's temperature-control system, which produces sweating to cool the body, stops working.

Signals of heat stroke are dry, hot, red skin; very high body temperature — sometimes as high as 106 degrees; progressive loss of consciousness; fast, weak pulse; and fast, shallow breathing.

First Aid

Heat stroke is a life-threatening situation. Call EMS or the Coast Guard immediately. Get the person out of the heat and into a cooler place. Cool

Normal

Heat Exhaustion

Heat Stroke

106°
98.6°

loss causes blood flow to decrease in the vital organs, resulting in a form of shock.

Signals of heat exhaustion are cool, moist, pale, or red skin; heavy sweating; dilated pupils; headache; nausea; dizziness and weakness; and exhaustion. Body temperature will be normal to below normal.

First Aid

Get the person out of the heat and into a cooler place. Place him or her on the back, with feet up. Either remove or loosen the victim's clothing. Cool him or her by fanning and applying cold packs (putting a cloth between the pack and the victim's skin) or wet towels or sheets. Care for shock. Give the victim one-half glass of water to drink every 15 minutes, if he or she is fully conscious and can tolerate it.

Heat Cramps

Heat cramps are muscular pains and spasms due to heavy exertion. They usually involve the abdominal muscles or legs. It is generally thought that the loss of water and salt from heavy sweating causes the cramps.

First Aid

As with heat emergencies, get the person to a cooler place. If the victim has no other injuries and can tolerate water, administer one-half glass every 15 minutes for an hour. Lightly stretch the muscle and gently massage the area. Watch the victim carefully after he or she begins to feel better.

the victim fast. Immerse him or her in cool water, or wrap wet sheets around the body and fan it. Care for shock while waiting for the Coast Guard or EMS to arrive. If the victim is conscious, offer cool water to drink.

Heat Exhaustion

Heat exhaustion is less dangerous than heat stroke. It typically occurs when people exercise heavily or work in a warm, humid place where body fluids are lost through heavy sweating. Fluid

Cold Emergencies

On days with low temperatures, high winds, and humidity, anyone can suffer from the extreme cold. Severe cold exposure can be life-threatening. Several factors increase the harmful effects of cold: being very young or very old, wearing wet clothing, having wounds or fractures, smoking, drinking alcoholic beverages, being fatigued, suffering emotional stress, and taking certain medications. People exposed to severe cold can suffer from hypothermia or frostbite.

Many times when people go into the water from a boat, it is unintentional. Cold water hitting the chest and back can activate the gasp reflex. If a person gasps while his/her head is under water, there is an obvious problem. Recovering from this initial shock may be difficult. Cold water can cause muscles to become stiff and make coordinated motion difficult. A prolonged stay in cold water following a capsizing or falling overboard may be deadly, even though the victim is able to overcome the initial shock. Water cools the body 25 times faster than air. Panic may set in and disorientation may result. Without a PFD, the person may head for the bottom.

By swimming or treading water, a person will cool about 35% faster than if remaining still. The "drownproofing technique" taught in many survival swimming classes requires putting the head into the water. Because the head is an area of high heat loss, drownproofing will cause a person to cool about 80% faster than if the head is kept out of the water. Drownproofing thus reduces survival time as much as one half in cold water. Do not drownproof in cold water!

The following table shows predicted survival times for an average person in 50-degree water.

PREDICTED SURVIVAL

SITUATION	TIME (hrs)
NO FLOTATION	
Drownproofing	1.5
Treading Water	2.0
WITH FLOTATION	
Swimming	2.0
Holding Still	2.7
H.E.L.P.	4.0
Huddle	4.0

predicted survival times for an average person in 50° water

Hypothermia

The signals of hypothermia include shivering, dizziness, numbness, confusion, weakness, impaired judgement, impaired vision, and drowsiness. The stages are —

1. Shivering.

2. Apathy.

3. Loss of consciousness.

4. Decreasing pulse rate and breathing rate.

5. Death.

As hypothermia progresses, the victim may move clumsily and have trouble holding objects; coordination may be impaired. In the later stages, he or she may stop shivering.

First Aid

Call the Coast Guard or EMS. Get a victim of hypothermia out of the cold and into dry clothing. Warm up his or her body slowly. Give nothing to eat or drink unless the victim is fully conscious. Monitor the <u>a</u>irway, <u>b</u>reathing, and <u>c</u>irculation (ABCs).

Frostbite

Frostbite is a common injury caused by exposure to cold. It happens when ice crystals form in body tissues, usually the nose, ears, chin, cheeks, fingers, or toes. This restricts blood flow to the injured parts. The effect is worse if the frostbitten parts are thawed and then frozen.

The first sign of frostbite may be that the skin is slightly flushed. The skin color of the frostbitten area then changes to white or grayish yellow and finally grayish blue, as the frostbite develops. Pain is sometimes felt early on but later goes away. The frostbitten part feels very cold and numb. The victim may not be aware of the injury.

Frostbite has degrees of tissue damage. Mild frostbite looks white or grayish, and the skin feels hard, even though the underlying tissue feels soft. In moderate frostbite, large blisters form on the surface and in the tissues underneath. The frostbitten area is hard, cold, and insensitive. If freezing is deeper than the skin, tissue damage is severe. Gangrene may result from the loss of blood supply to the area.

First Aid

Get the victim into a warm place. Put the frozen parts in warm (100-105 degrees) but not hot water. Handle them gently, and do not rub or massage them. If the toes or fingers are affected, put dry, sterile gauze between them after warming them. Loosely bandage the injured parts. If the part has been thawed and refrozen, then you should rewarm it at room temperature.

To learn more about first aid, every boater should take a CPR and/or First Aid course from the American Heart Association, American Red Cross, National Safety Council, or other nationally recognized organization.

Accidental Immersions

In case of accidental immersion into the water, remember that water conducts heat many times faster than air. Most boats will float even when capsized or swamped. Therefore, get in or on the boat to get as far out of the water as possible. This is true even if there is a cold wind blowing. There is always greater safety out of the water than in the water. Remember, a PFD will keep a victim afloat even if he or she is unconscious. Remaining still and, if possible, assuming the fetal or Heat Escape Lessening Posture (H.E.L.P.) will also increase the survival time. Since approximately 50% of body heat is lost from the head, it is

H.E.L.P. Position

important to remember to keep the head out of the water. Other areas of high heat loss are the neck, trunk, and groin.

NOTE: It is important to assume the H.E.L.P position while wearing a PFD. However, even a partial H.E.L.P. position gives some protection to the high head loss areas, thus increasing survival time.

HUDDLE position. The HUDDLE can be used with two or more people in the water. The important part of the procedure is to have the sides of the chest touching, if possible. Small children and older adults should be placed in the middle of the HUDDLE for more warmth.

HUDDLE Position

CARBON MONOXIDE

Boaters should be aware of the danger from carbon monoxide (CO) coming from internal combustion engines. Carbon monoxide is a colorless and odorless gas which is often undetected until too late. It causes headaches, nausea, vertigo, and death. People with cardiovascular problems are more susceptible to the gas.

Carbon monoxide can build up in any enclosed compartment, usually from a leak in the exhaust system. Additional ways it can build up are:

- Backdraft caused by a square stern can infiltrate a boat underway.

- Exhaust from a power generator can enter a boat through dry sink drains, especially on still days or when at anchor.

- Gasoline-powered inboard engines are potentially the most hazardous. When a boat is closed up tight with the engine running, the carburetor may pull the air out of the cabin, lowering the cabin air pressure. This in turn may draw carbon monoxide laden air into the cabin from outside.

Carbon monoxide can easily be purged from your boat if proper precautions are taken. When underway, run with an open hatch forward and an opening aft that will allow air to circulate through the boat from front to back. This will flush out carbon monoxide concentrations.

REMEMBER...

- Make sure that sink drains and other openings into the cabin are on the opposite side and as far away from any exhaust outlets as possible.

- Refrain from using the generator when anchored, tied up, or becalmed.

- Make sure the boat's ventilation system is unblocked and in good working order.

First Aid

All victims of inhaled poisons need oxygen as soon as possible. If it is possible to remove the person from the source of the poison without endangering another life, then do so. A conscious victim can be helped by just getting him or her to fresh air and then calling for medical assistance. Remove an unconscious victim from the environment, maintain an open airway, and call Coast Guard or EMS personnel immediately. If the person is not breathing, give rescue breathing.

REVIEW EXERCISE:

HYPOTHERMIA AND CARBON MONOXIDE

1. About _____ __ of body heat is lost from the head.

2. Carbon monoxide is hard to detect because it is _____ and _____.

3. Hypothermia victims should be treated gently and not allowed to _____.

SUMMARY

EMERGENCY PROCEDURES

In this chapter, you learned that if someone falls overboard, reach or throw something to them, but never go into the water unless appropriately trained and equipped. In addition, you learned the proper procedures to follow if a boat swamps, capsizes, catches on fire or runs aground.

There are basic procedures to follow if the boat becomes mechanically disabled while in the water. Spare parts and specific tools are essential to effect any repairs.

The basic techniques for rescue breathing and other first aid emergencies have been reviewed. By knowing how to use rescue breathing and how to deal with these special emergencies, the Skipper is better prepared to cope with and care for cardiac and other emergencies. Also, the importance of taking a first aid and CPR course from a nationally recognized training agency, such as the American Heart Association, American Red Cross, or National Safety Council was noted. And lastly, the use of distress signals and their application to enjoying a safe boating experience on the water was reviewed.

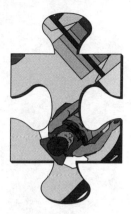

WHAT YOU WILL LEARN:

Fishing Rules

Waterskiing Rules

Hunting Rules

Water Activities

CHAPTER 11

INTRODUCTION

Waterborne hunting, fishing, and waterskiing, all add their own set of challenges and risks to the sport of boating. One major problem is that many do not view boating as the primary activity and neglect the navigation rules, courtesies, and safety precautions for safe boating. The purpose of this chapter is to consider what additional precautions need to be taken when boating around those participating in various water activities.

FISHING

In a recent survey, 50% of those who purchased boats said they bought them to go fishing. Unfortunately, approximately 1/3 of the national boating fatalities occurred while people were fishing from a boat. Many of these fatalities occurred when individuals who capsized their boats were either drunk or fell overboard while using the boats to hunt or fish.

When we see others fishing:

- Be careful to stay clear of fishing lines and nets.

- Slow down and reduce the wake of the boat so that it does not swamp or capsize other fishing vessels.

- Remember, damage caused by a boat's wake is the boat operator's responsibility.

When fishing from a boat:

- Don't stand up to fish unless absolutely sure that the boat will not capsize. And when choosing to stand, always wear a PFD.

- Be aware of other boats and wakes in the area so that there are no surprises.

- Never moor a boat to an aid to navigation (buoy) or anchor in a channel.

SAFETY TIP

Remember to protect exposed areas, such as face, neck, arms and legs from sunburn.

WATERSKIING

Waterskiing is an exciting and challenging sport. Pay special attention to the weather and other activity in the area when skiing. Keeping in mind these simple tips will help make skiing safe and fun.

The Ski Area

The size of the water area determines the number of boats and skiers that can safely operate within it simultaneously. Each boat should be able to maintain a 200-foot wide "ski corridor" (100 feet on either side of the boat). In order to avoid constant turning and risky maneuvering, the whole "ski course" should be at least 2000–3000 feet long.

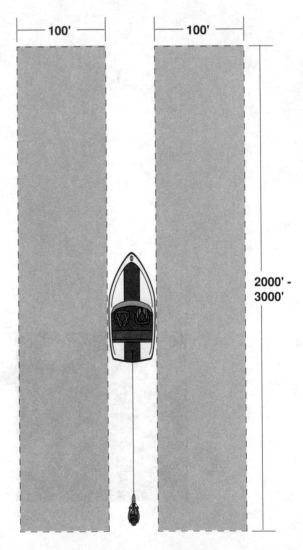

A minimum depth of six feet of obstacle free water is suggested for safe skiing in order to:

- Keep the skis from dragging bottom during starts, and

- Allow for a margin of safety against hitting the bottom or submerged obstacles during a fall.

Safety Tips for Waterskiers

Don't take unnecessary risks while waterskiing. Following the tips listed below will help a skier to safely enjoy this sport.

- Have an observer in the tow boat. This is a legal requirement in many states. The boat driver cannot watch the skier and maneuver the boat correctly at the same time. This is a three member team — skier, observer, and driver.

- Use a rear-view mirror.

- Wear a Coast Guard approved PFD designed for waterskiing. The observer and driver need PFDs also.

- Never ski in rough water. High waves or choppy water will prevent the tow boat from keeping a steady course and speed, hence fatiguing the skier.

- Stay well clear of congested areas and obstructions. Waterskiing requires a lot of room. Keep away from crowded beaches, docks, swim areas, rocks and bridge pilings.

- Don't spray swimmers, boats or other skiers. Such stunts are dangerous as well as discourteous.

- Never ski after dark. It is hazardous AND illegal. Any boat traveling fast enough to tow a skier is traveling too fast to navigate safely at night.

- NEVER waterski and/or operate a boat while under the influence of alcohol or drugs. Such activity is extremely dangerous because of the impairment to judgment and reflexes. A recent study conducted with expert skiers who were deliberately intoxicated indicated that even their ability to ski was dramatically reduced.

- Use hand signals between the skier and observer. Before starting, go over the meaning of each signal to eliminate confusion during skiing.

The boat operator should navigate safely in a designated waterskiing zone, and NEVER go near shore, swimming areas, or close to fishermen or other boats. The boat should not make sharp turns. The

❶ OK
❷ OK
❸ Finished/ Retrieve Me
❹ Slower
❺ Turn Right
❻ Turn Left
❼ Faster
❽ OK
❾ Stop

HAND SIGNALS

11•3

towline should be at least 75-feet long. A rule of thumb for safety's sake is to always keep the skier at least twice the length of the tow line from any potential hazards at all times.

While many areas with obstacles are marked by warning buoys or signs, it is up to the boat operator, observer and skier to be alert to any potential hazards (marked and unmarked) in the skiing area.

Remember:

- Avoid solid objects when landing. Many serious injuries occur when skiers attempt to stop near floats, piers or pilings.

- Ski in familiar areas. Consult charts of the area, ask other skiers who possess "local knowledge," and personally drive the boat through the course before actually skiing it.

- Protect yourself against sunburn.

Retrieving a Skier

Falling down in the water while waterskiing is a common occurrence, especially for beginners. If the skier falls or makes a water landing, return to pick him up as soon as possible, since a fallen skier is difficult for other boats to see. The skier in the water should hold up a ski to improve his visibility in the water and to signal that he is ok.

The boat operator reduces speed immediately while the observer maintains visual contact with the skier and directs the operator. As the boat returns to pick up the fallen skier, the operator continues to reduce the speed and eventually shuts the engine off.

Weather

Be aware of the effects of cold weather and cold water. Loss of body heat leads to a reduction in coordination and judgment. The use of wetsuits is an effective way to reduce the chilling effects of wind and cold weather. However, even a wetsuit has limitations. Do not jeopardize a skier's safety by prolonging their exposure to cold weather or cold water.

Skiing in rain is not recommended because of the loss of visibility experienced by the boat operator and skier. Skiing in lightning is extremely dangerous to both the occupants in the boat and the skier.

OBSERVER SIGNALS DRIVER & MAINTAINS VISUAL CONTACT WITH FALLEN SKIER

FALLEN SKIER

TURN OFF MOTOR

REDUCE TO IDLE

HUNTING

Each year more hunters die from drowning and the effects of hypothermia than from gunshot wounds. Many waterborne hunting accidents occur when a hunter reaches for a decoy, capsizes the boat from an unbalanced load, or falls overboard due to intoxication. Keep in mind that many hunters do not regard themselves as "boaters," and as a consequence do not consider the special conditions and challenges of the marine environment. Remember to leave a float plan with a responsible person.

Below are some pointers to consider when hunting on the water.

The Boat

Be familiar with the characteristics of the boat. Most hunters use smaller craft such as johnboats, bassboats, or canoes because of their portability. Because many of these boats have flat bottoms or narrow beams, they are more prone to swamping or capsizing if used unsafely.

Remember:

- **NEVER** drink alcohol and boat.

- Never cross large bodies of water during rough weather.

- Don't overload a boat with passengers or equipment. Stow items low and in the center of the boat.

- Avoid standing up or moving around. This includes dogs as well. Always remain seated when shooting.

- Stay with the boat if it capsizes. Don't try getting to shore. The distance may be greater than it appears.

The Environment

The weather and surrounding water conditions are important factors to consider when setting out on a hunting trip. Most waterborne hunting fatalities occur on smaller bodies of water late in the year. This is when water and air temperatures are lower, and there is a greater frequency of storms. If the weather looks bad or there is a forecast for upcoming storms, don't risk going out!

REVIEW EXERCISE:
WATER ACTIVITIES

1. Waterskiing involves a 3-person team — the skier, the _____, and the _____.

2. When recovering skiers from the water, be sure the engine is _____.

3. When hunting from a boat, remain _____ when shooting.

4. As a hunter, it is doubly important to leave a _____ with a responsible person.

SUMMARY

WATER ACTIVITIES

This chapter on Water Activities covered the areas of fishing, waterskiing, and hunting. Even though those out fishing and hunting may not consider themselves as boaters, they are still subject to the rules and requirements established for recreational boating.

- Remember, when fishing, stay clear of lines and nets.

- Be considerate of others around the area when anchoring.

- Waterskiing safely requires at least three persons: the skier, the operator and the observer.

- You may be exposed for prolonged periods to sun, wind, and possibly rain or cold temperatures. What will keep you comfortable so you can be attentive while operating your boat? (sun screen, a hat, sunglasses, foul weather gear...)

- Familiarize yourself with the various characteristics of your boat. Don't overload the boat, and avoid standing up or moving around in the boat.

In all these activities — hunting, fishing, and waterskiing — the participants must be weather conscious. Hold off a few hours or a day to make sure the weather will cooperate. Even though a little rain never hurt anyone, it can cause problems on the water.

WHAT YOU WILL LEARN:

Classes of Trailers

Basics of Trailering

Towing Precautions

Things to Remember

Trailering Your Boat

CHAPTER 12

INTRODUCTION

More than 90% of the boats in this country are trailerable. This allows many boaters to tow their boats long distances and enjoy waters far from home. Whether the trip is short or long, trailering a boat requires knowledge of trailer safety and proper operation.

When trailering a boat, you must conform to highway motor vehicle laws. Be certain the trailer and vehicle equipment meets the legal requirements. When registering the trailer, consult the state police or the motor vehicle bureau of the state or states where the boat may be towed.

Successful trailering requires four things: the proper trailer, the right hitch, an adequately powered tow vehicle, and a properly loaded trailer. One must also learn how to launch and retrieve the boat with a trailer.

To insure that the boat and trailer are compatible, check with the boat or trailer manufacturer or dealer.

This chapter will discuss a few basic requirements for trailering.

TRAILER CLASSIFICATION

Trailers are divided into classes based on the total weight of the trailer and its load. The load includes all the miscellaneous gear which is stowed in the boat, such as the motor, fuel tank(s), fishing gear, and required safety equipment.

The maximum width that a trailer and boat may be is 8.5 feet, unless the operator has a special permit.

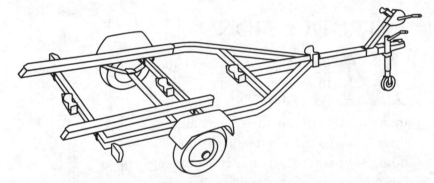

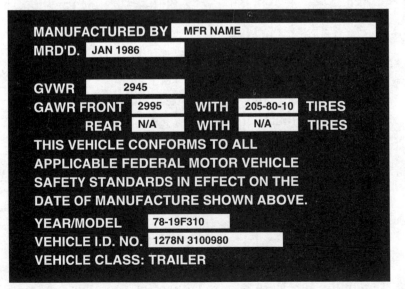

MANUFACTURED BY	MFR NAME			
MRD'D.	JAN 1986			
GVWR	2945			
GAWR FRONT	2995	WITH	205-80-10	TIRES
REAR	N/A	WITH	N/A	TIRES

THIS VEHICLE CONFORMS TO ALL APPLICABLE FEDERAL MOTOR VEHICLE SAFETY STANDARDS IN EFFECT ON THE DATE OF MANUFACTURE SHOWN ABOVE.

YEAR/MODEL	78-19F310
VEHICLE I.D. NO.	1278N 3100980

VEHICLE CLASS: TRAILER

Capacity Information

The Capacity Rating of the trailer should be greater than the combined weight of the boat, motor, and equipment. Federal law requires that all trailers have certain important capacity information displayed. The Gross Vehicle Weight Rating (GVWR) for the trailer must be displayed, which includes the trailer and all weight it is expected to carry. The Gross Axle Weight Rating (GAWR) capacity information specifies the proper tires needed to carry the load for which the trailer is rated. On multi-axle trailers, the combined GAWR of all axles must be equal to or greater than the GVWR for the trailer.

Weight

Safe trailering requires that the trailer be properly balanced and loaded. Overloading a trailer on the highway may be as dangerous as overloading a boat on the water. The trailer-boater needs to know two important weights: gross vehicle weight and tongue weight.

Gross Vehicle Weight

To determine the gross vehicle (trailer) weight, load the trailer with everything that normally would be on it during transportation. Take the rig to the nearest scale that has a platform, such as a highway weighing station, and weigh the rig without the towing vehicle, unhitched and supported on a jack. This will give the gross trailer weight. It is important that the gross trailer weight (Gross Vehicle Weight) does not exceed the Gross Vehicle Weight Rating as shown on the capacity label. Keep the trailer in a level position by adjusting the jack-caster assembly.

The gross weight of the trailer may be reduced by carrying only light items such as sleeping bags on the boat, and placing heavy items, such as canned goods, in the tow vehicle. The amount of fuel and any water in the boat (from rain, for example) may add substantially to the trailer's gross weight and play havoc with the load distribution. Pull out the boat's drainplug to make certain there is no water in the boat before towing.

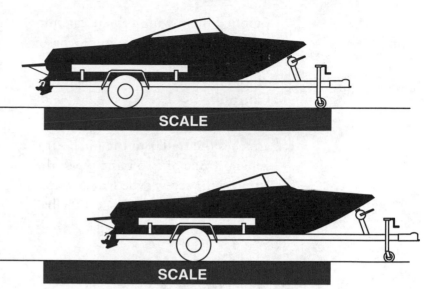

Tongue Weight

The difference between the Gross Trailer Weight and the Gross Axle Weight is the Tongue Weight. In loading the trailer, it is important that the weight distribution on the trailer is such that the recommended tongue weight is maintained.

The Hitch

Choosing the proper class of hitch for the weight of the trailer being towed is very important. There are two basic types of hitches, the weight carrying hitch and the weight distribution (or load equalizer) hitch.

Hitch classes

The class of hitch required will depend on the gross trailer weight and its tongue weight. The dealer that

CHOOSING THE RIGHT HITCH

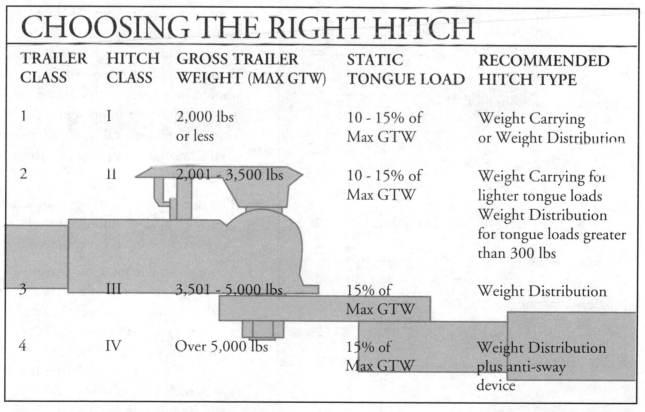

TRAILER CLASS	HITCH CLASS	GROSS TRAILER WEIGHT (MAX GTW)	STATIC TONGUE LOAD	RECOMMENDED HITCH TYPE
1	I	2,000 lbs or less	10 - 15% of Max GTW	Weight Carrying or Weight Distribution
2	II	2,001 - 3,500 lbs	10 - 15% of Max GTW	Weight Carrying for lighter tongue loads Weight Distribution for tongue loads greater than 300 lbs
3	III	3,501 - 5,000 lbs	15% of Max GTW	Weight Distribution
4	IV	Over 5,000 lbs	15% of Max GTW	Weight Distribution plus anti-sway device

supplied the towing vehicle can normally provide guidance in purchasing a suitable hitch.

Coupler

The coupler is the mechanism which attaches the trailer to the hitch. It is generally one of two basic types, the latch or the screw type which keeps the coupler from coming off the ball hitch.

Latch Type Coupler

REVIEW EXERCISE:

TRAILER CLASSIFICATION

1. Successful trailering requires 4 things:
   _____,
   _____,
   _____,
   and_____.

2. It is important to have the proper trailer for the boat to prevent _____ to the hull.

3. There are two basic types of hitches, the _____ and the _____.

4. There are two basic coupler types, the _____ or the _____ type.

5. The Tongue Weight of a trailer is the difference between the _____ and the _____.

TRAILERING THE BOAT

Choose the proper trailer for the boat. More damage can be done to a boat by the stresses of road travel than by normal water operation. A boat hull is designed to be supported evenly by water. When transported on a trailer, the boat should be supported structurally as evenly across the hull as possible. This will allow for even distribution of the weight of the hull, engine and equipment. It should be long enough to support the whole length of the hull, but short enough to allow the lower unit of the boat's engine to be extended freely.

- Rollers and bolsters must be kept in good condition to prevent scratching and gouging of the hull.

- Tie-downs and lower unit supports must be adjusted properly to prevent the boat from bouncing on the trailer. The bow eye on the boat should be secured with either a rope, chain or turnbuckle in addition to the winch cable. Additional straps may be required across the beam of the boat.

- The capacity of the trailer should be greater than the combined weight of the boat, motor, and equipment.

- The tow vehicle must be capable of handling the weight of the trailer, (with boat and equipment) as well as the weight of the passengers and equipment which will be carried inside. This may require that the tow vehicle be specially equipped with the following:

*(CHECK YOUR VEHICLE OWN-
ERS MANUAL FOR SPECIFIC
INFORMATION)*

- Engine of adequate power.

- Transmission and rear-end designed
  for towing.

- Larger cooling systems for the
  engine and transmission.

- Heavy duty brakes.

- Load bearing hitch attached to the
  frame, not the bumper.

Check These Items Before Trailering On The Highway:

- The tow ball and coupler are the
  same size and bolts with washers are
  tightly secured. *(The vibration of
  road travel can loosen them.)*

- The coupler is completely over the
  ball and the latching mechanism is
  locked down and secured.

- The trailer is loaded evenly from
  front to rear as well as side to side.
  Too much weight on the hitch will
  cause the rear wheels of the tow
  vehicle to drag and may make
  steering more difficult.

- Too much weight on the rear of the
  trailer will cause the trailer to
  "fishtail" and may reduce traction
  or even lift the rear wheels of the
  tow vehicle off the ground. Be
  particularly careful of water in the
  boat.

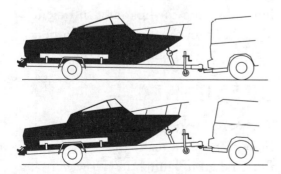

- The safety chains are attached,
  crisscrossing under the coupler, to
  the frame of the tow vehicle. If the
  ball were to break, the tongue
  would be held up by the chains,
  allowing the trailer to follow in a
  straight line and prevent the coupler
  from dragging on the road.

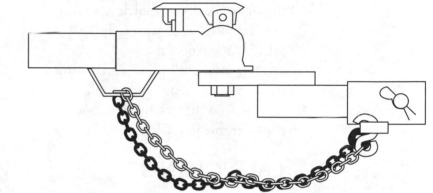

- The lights on the trailer function
  properly.

- Check the brakes. On a level
  parking area, roll forward and
  apply the brakes several times at
  increasing speeds to determine a
  safe stopping distance. (Do not tow
  any trailer faster than 55 mph —
  some states, 45 mph.)

- The side-view mirrors of towing
  vehicle are large enough to provide
  an unobstructed rear view on both
  sides of the vehicle.

- Check tires (including spare) and
  wheel bearings. Improper inflation
  may cause difficulty in steering.
  When trailer wheels are immersed
  in water, (especially salt water) the
  bearings should be inspected and
  greased on a regular basis.

- Rainwater or water from cleaning is
  undesirable for many reasons, but
  mainly because a collection of it can
  rapidly increase weight on the
  trailer, often beyond its capacity.
  This extra weight may shift with the
  movement of the trailer and cause a
  dangerous situation.

12•5

Towing Precautions

Pulling a trailer presents problems: more time is required to brake, accelerate, pass, and stop. The turning radius is also much greater; curbs and roadside barriers must be given a wide berth when negotiating corners. It is suggested that prior to operating on the open road, the vehicle operator practice turning, backing up, and other maneuvers on a level, uncongested parking area. Backing a trailer is a challenge even to the most experienced drivers and requires considerable practice.

LAUNCHING

For the courtesy of others and to prevent rushing, prepare the boat for launching away from the ramp.

- Check the boat to insure that no damage was caused by the trip.

- Raise the lower unit of the motor (remove supports) to the proper height for launching so that it will not hit bottom.

- Make sure the drain plug is in securely.

- Remove tie downs and make sure that the winch is properly attached to the bow eye and locked in position.

- Disconnect the trailer lights to prevent shorting the electrical system or burning out a bulb.

- Attach a line to the bow and the stern of the boat so that the boat cannot drift away after launching and can be easily maneuvered to a docking area.

- Visually inspect the launch ramp for hazards such as a steep drop off, slippery area and sharp objects.

When everything has been double checked, proceed slowly to the ramp remembering that the boat is just resting on the trailer and attached only at the bow. The ideal situation is to have one person in the boat and one observer at the water's edge to help guide the driver of the tow vehicle.

When launching:

- Keep the rear wheels of the tow vehicle out of the water. This will generally keep the exhaust pipes out of the water. If the exhaust pipes become immersed in the water, the engine may stall.

- Set the parking brake and place tire chocks behind rear wheels.

- Make sure someone else on shore is holding the lines attached to the boat.

- Once in the water, lower the motor (be certain there is sufficient depth as not to damage the prop) and prepare to start the engine (after running blowers and checking for fuel leaks).

- Start the boat motor and make sure that water is passing through the engine cooling system.

- Release the winch and disconnect the winch line from the bow when the boat operator is ready.

At this point, the boat can be launched with a light shove or by backing off the trailer under power. Finish loading the boat at a sufficient distance from the ramp so that others may use the launch ramp.

RETRIEVAL

The steps for removing the boat from the water are basically the reverse of those taken to launch it. However, keep in mind that certain conditions may exist during retrieval that did not exist during launching. When approaching the takeout ramp, take special care to note such factors as:

- Change in wind direction and/or velocity.

- Change in current and/or tide.

- Change in water level due to tide.

- Increase in boating traffic.

- Visibility, etc.

First, unload the boat at a dock or mooring if possible. Next, maneuver the boat carefully to the submerged trailer; stop the engine and raise the lower unit of the engine. Secure engine; then winch the boat onto the trailer and secure it. Finally, drive the trailer with boat aboard carefully from the ramp to a designated parking area for cleanup, reloading, and an equipment safety check. Practice will make launching and retrieving a simple procedure. The best advice is just, "do it cautiously with safety as a main concern." **Avoid being rushed by impatient boaters.**

STORAGE

Since the boat may be sitting on its trailer for quite some time before it is used again, it is important that it be stored properly. To avoid damage from sun and weather, cover the boat with a tarp. To remove weight from the wheels, place a cinderblock or wood beams under the tongue and under the trailer frame.

Rules of Operation

CHAPTER 13

INTRODUCTION

Previous chapters discussed boat requirements, legal requirements, the weather warning, navigation rules, and emergency procedures. It is also important to understand the rules of operation. This chapter will cover these often neglected areas which may seem redundant, but are very important. Negligent operation, defensive boating, boating while under the influence, accidents and reporting safety defects fall under this heading.

ON-THE-SPOT CORRECTIONS

Under Public Law 98-89, the Coast Guard, while observing a boat operating in an unsafe condition on federal waters (say, grossly overloaded), can "terminate" that boat's trip by directing the operator to the nearest dock (or safe area) and have it stay there until the condition is corrected.

13•1

NEGLIGENT OR GROSSLY NEGLIGENT OPERATION

If a Marine Law Enforcement Official observes a boat being operated in a negligent manner (for example, pulling a water skier through a busy swimming area), it could result in a fine or jail! The difference between negligent and grossly negligent operation is a matter of the operator's knowledge of the risk of harm. Speeding in an obviously posted swimming area could be viewed as grossly negligent and could result in either a fine, jail, or both. The boat operator is responsible for learning and observing all rules and regulations regarding the safe operation of a boat — so study them carefully.

DEFENSIVE BOATING

Safe boating involves the ability to operate a boat in such a manner as to avoid being involved in a PREVENTABLE accident. Like other accidents, most of those involving boats are

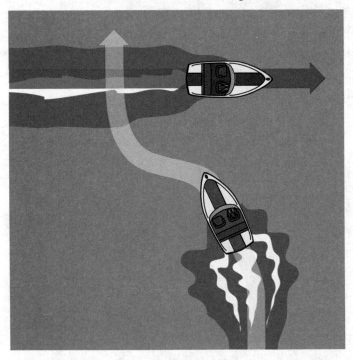

preventable. Defensive operation is the key to safe boating. Defensive boating is the prevention of accidents in spite of the actions of others or the presence of adverse conditions. If another boater creates a hazardous situation, it may be necessary to depart from standard procedures under the navigation rules just to avoid an accident. In fact, such a situation is recognized and such a departure from standard procedures is authorized under both the International and Inland Rules of the Road. These decisions require alertness and good judgment on the operator's part, much the same as driving on the highway. Keep a proper lookout!

BOATING AND ALCOHOL

We have discussed some of the requirements for the boat that will help make a safe outing. A factor often overlooked is the condition of the boat operator. The most seaworthy and best equipped boat will be next to useless if the skipper is not "ALERT."

Just a few hours of sun, wind, glare, noise, vibration, and motion can tire boat operators enough to allow them to miss important things around them which could cause or prevent an accident. Operators need to be aware of this and make a special effort to be alert at all times.

In addition, any alcohol consumed will interact with this fatigue, and the combined effects of alcohol and fatigue result in impaired judgment and slowed reflexes. Responsible boat operators save their drinking until they get home.

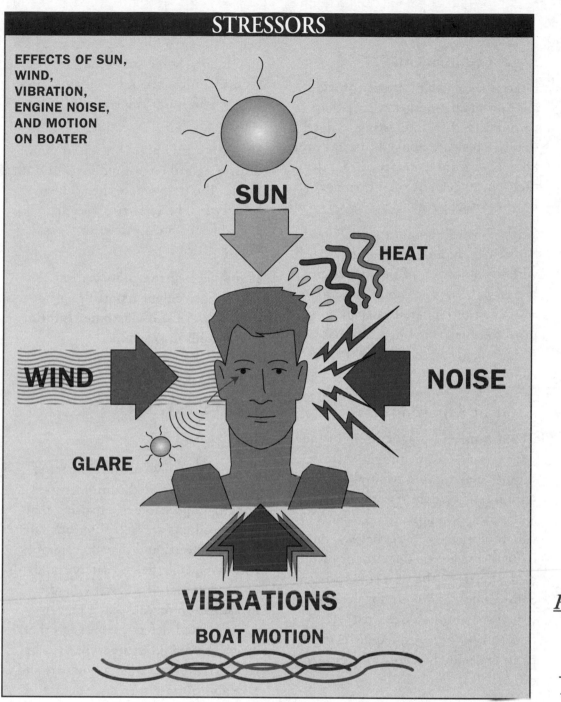

STRESSORS

EFFECTS OF SUN, WIND, VIBRATION, ENGINE NOISE, AND MOTION ON BOATER

SUN

HEAT

WIND

NOISE

GLARE

VIBRATIONS

BOAT MOTION

REMEMBER:

ALCOHOL + FATIGUE = DISASTER

It is important to remember, too, that operating a boat while under the influence of alcohol on federal waters is a Federal offense, punishable by a civil fine of up to $1,000, a criminal fine of up to $5,000, imprisonment for not more than one year, or a combination of fine and imprisonment. Also, many states are enacting or toughening "Boating Under the Influence" laws.

REVIEW EXERCISE:

DRINKING AND BOATING

1. Name the five contributing factors that can tire a boat operator _____, _____, _____, _____, _____.

2. Operating a vessel while under the influence of alcohol is a _____.

ACCIDENTS

Legal Requirements

Boaters, as a group, usually provide aid during an emergency situation voluntarily. It is interesting to note that skippers are obliged to assist other boaters in trouble provided that they, their passengers, or their own boat are not put in jeopardy.

Skippers who respond to the "Good Samaritan" requirement in good faith, without objection of the distressed individual, are not liable for damages as a result of rendered assistance, provided they acted in a reasonable and prudent manner under the circumstances.

Accident Reporting

By learning and practicing all of the safety points in this program, the skipper may never have to fill out and send in an accident report. However, all boating accidents (or accidents which meet the criteria below), must be reported by the operator or owner of the vessel to the proper marine law enforcement authority for the state in which the accident occurred. The following conditions require filing a boating accident report (See Appendix F):

• When a life is lost due to the accident (immediate notification is required);

• When someone is injured and requires medical attention beyond first aid (report must be filed within 48 hours);

• When damage to the vessel and other property totals more than $500 or there is complete loss of the boat (report must be made within 10 days of incident).

If these seem general to you, remember it is best to file a report if you have any doubt. Some states may require reports for less serious accidents, so be sure to check out the laws within the state.

When filing an accident report, you must obtain the required form and file it with the state where the accident occurred. The reporting form is available at state agencies or Coast Guard offices.

If you need further information regarding accident reporting, please call the U.S.C.G. Customer Infoline, 1-800-368-5647.

REPORTING POSSIBLE BOAT SAFETY DEFECTS

According to law, manufacturers of boats and associated equipment are directly responsible for assuring that their products are free of serious safety related defects, and that they comply with applicable federal safety standards or regulations. If a Coast Guard investigation reveals that a reported safety related defect extends to other boats, the manufacturer will then be REQUIRED to notify all owners and take appropriate corrective action. If a serious problem, which may be the result of a defect in design or construction, occurs, contact the U.S.C.G. Customer Infoline at 1-800-368-5647. This shared information may prevent serious boating accidents from endangering other boaters.

REVIEW EXERCISE: ACCIDENTS

1. Skippers are _____ to help other boaters in trouble.

2. Name the conditions that require an accident report to be filed. _____.

SUMMARY

RULES OF OPERATION

This chapter reviewed important, but sometimes neglected areas of on-the-spot corrections, negligent operation, defensive boating, drinking alcohol while boating, accidents and reports, and boat defects.

The Coast Guard can "terminate" a boating trip if there is an unsafe condition or for negligent operation, such as skiing in a swimming area, overloading beyond manufacturer's recommended safe loading capacity, etc. These conditions are dangerous to boaters and others enjoying the water.

Defensive boating follows and encourages boaters to operate a boat so as to prevent accidents. One significant cause of boating accidents is drinking alcohol. Wind, noise, sun, vibration, and glare can cause fatigue on the water. Add alcohol to those stressors, and the boat operators lose their quick reflexes. Besides, operating under the influence of alcohol and/or drugs is against the law.

Next, the chapter explained which accidents the Skipper is required to report. Remember the timelines that govern report filing.

The last item in this chapter was reporting possible boat safety defects. Keep the U.S.C.G. Customer Infoline number handy (1-800-368-5647).

APPENDIX A

REVIEW EXERCISES

Exercise Page		Answer Page
2.14	1. a. coastal waters; the Great Lakes; territorial seas	[2.12]
	b. motor	[2.12]
	c. 16	[2.12]
	2. three	[2.13]
	3. three short, three long, three short	[2.14]
	4. hot slag will not drip on the boater or the boat	[2.13]
2.18	1. sunset; sunrise; reduced visibility	[2.15]
	2. 1. red	[2.15]
	2. green	[2.15]
	3. white	[2.15]
	4. yellow	[2.15]
	3. 1. masthead 225	[2.15]
	2. all-round 360	[2.15]
	3. sidelights 112.5	[2.15]
	4. sternlight 135	[2.15]
	4. white (and/or yellow if towing)	[2.15-16]
	5. a.	[combo]
2.19	1. 1-4 portable fuel tanks; anchor and anchor line; backup propulsion; spare parts; hull repair kits; bailers; miscellaneous equipment	[2.18-19]
	2. five; ten	[2.19]
	3. False	[2.19]
3.5	1. plastic	[3.2-3]
	2. waste management plan	
	3. size of boat; available space/power; system flexibility, ease of conversion or modification	[3.4]
4.5	1. go	[combo]
	2. local newspaper; NOAA weather broadcasts; Coast Guard; television and/or cable TV	[4.2]
	3. storm moving into the area	[4.2]
	4. grounding system; electrical conductor	[4.3]
	5. bow; into	[4.4]
5.2	1. when; where; when; who	[5.2]
	2. a responsible person	[5.2]
	3. the Coast Guard	[5.2]
5.6	1. removed from the boat	[5.5]
	2. get everyone out of the boat (secure the boat; close ports, windows, doors; check how much fuel the tank will take); engines, motors, fans, fires	[5.5]
	3. in contact with the tank opening	[5.5]

6.5	1. two; two	[6.2]
	2. one short blast, to turn right, pass port to port	[6.2-3]
	3. give way; stand on; slow and/or change course;	
	maintain course and speed	[6.4]
	4. give way; stand on; one; one	[6.4]
	5. two; five or more; remain in position	[6.4]
7.3	1. danger	[7.2]
	2. control (regulation)	[7.3]
	3. information	[7.3]
7.5	1. can; green; odd	[7.4]
	2. nun; red; even	[7.4]
	3. lighted; red and white striped, red or green;	
	red, green or whitelights	[7.4-5]
	4. left	[7.4]
	5. right	[7.4]
9.3	1. direction	[9.2]
	2. rear	[9.1]
9.7	1. side of the bow	[9.5-6]
	2. neutral; drift	[9.5]
	3. cleat hitch	[9.6]
9.9	1. wind; current	[9.8]
	2. bow; stern line	[9.8]
	3. veer off or stop to avoid collision;	
	do not assume the other skipper sees your boat.	[9.8]
9.10	1. be certain everyone is wearing a PFD and	
	it is securely fastened	[9.10]
	2. slightly on one side or the other	[9.10]
	3. following	[9.10]
10.5	1. fall overboard	[10.2]
	2. maintain constant watch on the person overboard	[10.2]
	3. stay	[10.5]
	4. f	[combo]
10.7	1. paddle; boat hook	[10.6]
	2. move and shift their weight	[10.7]
	3. checking; PFD	[10.6]

Exercise Page		Answer Page
10.9	1. a. drive train	[10.7]
	b. electrical ignition system	[10.7]
	c. fuel	[10.7]
	2. serious damage to the engine	[10.7]
10.11	1. Mayday - Mayday - Mayday	[10.11]
	2. arm waving	[10.10]
10.19	1. 50%	[10.17]
	2. colorless; odorless	[10.18]
	3. eat or drink (unless fully conscious)	[10.17]
11.5	1. observer; boat operator	[11.3]
	2. off	[11.4]
	3. seated	[11.5]
	4. float plan	[11.5]
12.4	1. the proper trailer, the right hitch, an adequately powered tow vehicle, and a properly loaded trailer	[12.1]
	2. damage	[12.4]
	3. weight carrying hitch; weight distribution	[12.3]
	4. latch; screw	[12.4]
	5. Gross Trailer Weight; Gross Axle Weight	[12.3]
12.7	1. crisscrossing	[12.5]
	2. chocks	[12.6]
	3. release	[12.6]
	4. fishtail; traction	[12.5]
	5. in the boat; at the water's edge	[12.7]
13.3	1. effects of sun, wind, vibration, engine noise, motion on boater	[13.3]
	2. Federal offense	[13.3]
13.5	1. obliged	[13.4]
	2. when life is lost; medical attention beyond first aid; damage to the vessel and other property exceeds $500; a complete loss of the boat	[13.4]

USCG AUXILIARY

The U.S. Coast Guard Auxiliary is a volunteer, non-military organization comprised of owners of boats, aircraft, and amateur radio stations. Its 36,000 members receive no pay for their services.

The Auxiliary is established by law to assist the regular Coast Guard in promoting safety and efficiency in the operation of pleasure craft. To accomplish this, it carries out three basic programs: Public Instruction, Courtesy Marine Examination and Operations.

U.S. COAST GUARD AUXILIARY PUBLIC EDUCATION COURSES

The U.S. Coast Guard Auxiliary has offered courses in boating safety and seamanship to the public since 1953. During the last five years, they have expanded boating courses from three to eight. The courses are taught by experienced, qualified Auxiliary members. The only charge to the student is for administration or course materials. Contact your local auxiliary flotilla, or watch for notices in your newspaper for information. The courses offered are:

1. *Boating Skills and Seamanship (BS&S)*

There are 6 to 13 lessons for the general boating audience. One of the U.S. Coast Guard Auxiliary's two in-depth courses. Certificates are awarded to graduates. Coverage exceeds minimum National Association of State Boating Law Administrators (NASBLA) standards and is accepted by all states. This course should be offered at least once each year by all flotillas.

2. *Sailing and Seamanship (S&S)*

The other U.S. Coast Guard Auxiliary's in-depth course. This is a 7-to-14 lesson course. Certificates are awarded to graduates. Similar coverage as BS&S, but designed for sailors.

3. *Basic Coastal Navigation (BCN)*

Six to eight lessons for students who enjoyed the Piloting Chapter in the BS&S or S&S course.

4. *Advanced Coastal Navigation (ACN)*

This is a 12+ lesson course for BS&S, S&S, or similar course graduates. For students interested in a challenging course.

5. *Boats 'N' Kids (BNK)*

One-lesson course geared to children in the second through about fourth grade (ages 7 to 10). An introduction to boating safety for children.

6. *Water 'N' Kids (WNK)*

One-lesson course geared to children in kindergarten through second or third grade (ages 5 to 8). A good course for children.

7. *It's a Boat, Skipper (PWC—Personal Watercraft Course)*

One-lesson, "stand-alone" introductory boating safety course for PWC operators, or as an additional lesson of a BS&S or BSC course.

8. *Boating Safely (BSC)*

Four lessons offered by both the U.S. Coast Guard Auxiliary and the U.S. Power Squadrons as a basic, NASBLA-approved course.

APPENDIX C

USCG AUXILIARY DISTRICT OFFICES

Director of Auxiliary
First Coast Guard Dist. (NR)
408 Atlantic Avenue
Boston, MA 02210

Asst. Director of Auxiliary
First Coast Guard Dist. (NR)
Otis Air Natl. Guard Base, MA 02542

Director of Auxiliary
First Coast Guard Dist. (SR)
Bldg. 400, Section C, Rm. 103
Governors Island
New York, NY 10004

Director of Auxiliary
Second Coast Guard Dist. (ER)
4335 River Rd.
Cincinnati, OH 45204

Director of Auxiliary
Second Coast Guard Dist. (NR)
P.O. 46
Ft. Snelling, MN 55111

Director of Auxiliary
Second Coast Guard Dist. (SR)
220 Great Cr. Rd., #148
Nashville, TN 37228

Director of Auxiliary
Second Coast Guard Dist. (WR)
1222 Spruce St., 1.103
St. Louis, MO 63103

Director of Auxiliary
Fifth Coast Guard Dist. (NR)
1 Washington Ave. #202
Philadelphia, PA 19147

Director of Auxiliary
Fifth Coast Guard Dist. (SR)
431 Crawford St.
Portsmouth, VA 23705

Director of Auxiliary
Seventh Coast Guard Dist.
Fed. Bldg. 909, SE 1st Ave.
Miami, FL 33131

Director of Auxiliary
Eighth Coast Guard Dist.
501 Magazine St.
New Orleans, LA 70130

Director of Auxiliary
Ninth Coast Guard Dist. (CR)
650 S. Harbor Drive
Grand Haven, MI 49417

Director of Auxiliary
Ninth Coast Guard Dist. (ER)
1 Fuhrman Blvd.
Buffalo, NY 12403

Director of Auxiliary
Ninth Coast Guard Dist. (WR)
2420 S. Lincoln Mem.
Milwaukee, WI 53207

Director of Auxiliary (NR)
Eleventh Coast Guard Dist.
Coast Guard Island
Alameda, CA 94501

Director of Auxiliary (SR)
Eleventh Coast Guard Dist.
501 W. Ocean Blvd., Rm. 6100
Long Beach, CA 90822-5399

Director of Auxiliary
Thirteenth Coast Guard Dist.
915 2nd Ave., Fed. Bldg.
Seattle, WA 98174

Director of Auxiliary
Fourteenth Coast Guard Dist.
300 Ala Moana Blvd.
Honolulu, HI 96850

Director of Auxiliary
Seventeenth Coast Guard Dist.
PO Box 25517
Juneau, AK 99802

APPENDIX D

USCG DISTRICT OFFICES

Atlantic
Governor's Island
New York, NY 10004-5098
(212) 668-7196

Pacific
Coast Guard Island
Alameda, CA 94501-5100
(415) 437-3196

United States Coast Guard District Map

United States Coast Guard Districts

District Offices	Jurisdictions
CDR, 1st CG Dist. (b)	
408 Atlantic Ave.	All New England to Tom's
Boston MA 02110-3350	River, NJ, and part of NY
Phone: (617) 223-8515	
Fax: (617) 223-8523	
E-mail: DPA/D1D2	
CRD, 5th CG Dist. (ba)	
431 Crawford St.	MD, DE, Washington DC,
Portsmouth VA 23704-5004	VA, NC, and parts of NJ
Phone: (804) 398-6272	and PA
Fax: (804) 398-6238	
E-mail: DPA/D5D	
CDR, 7th CG Dist. (b)	
909 S.E. 1st Ave.	SC, GA, most of FL,
Puerto	
Miami FL 33131-3050	Rico and adjacent U.S.
Phone: (305) 536-5641	islands
Fax: (305) 536-7402	
E-mail: DPA/D725	
CDR, 8th CG Dist. (b)	
501 Magazine St.	Mississippi River system,
New Orleans LA 70130-3396	the Illinois River north of
Phone: (504) 589-6198	Joliet; western Fl and GA;
Fax: (504) 589 2142	AL; MS; LA; TX; and NM
E-mail: DPA/D8D	*The 2nd and 8th districts recently were combined.
CDR, 9th CG Dist. (b)	
1240 E. 9th St.	MI, parts of OH, IL, IN,
MN,	
Cleveland OH 44199-2060	WI, NY and PA
Phone: (216) 522-3900	
Fax: (216) 522-4447	
E-mail: CPO D Schaefer/D9D	

District Offices	Jurisdictions
CDR, 11th CG Dist. (ba)	
Coast Guard Pacific Area/	CA, AZ, NV and UT
Maritime Defense	
Zone Pacific/11th CG District	
Coast Guard Island	
Alameda CA 99501-5100	
Phone: (510) 437-3324/5	
Fax: (510) 437-5918	
E-mail: ADMIN/D11DPANR	
CDR, 13th CG Dist. (ba)	
915 Second Ave., Suite #3352	OR, WA, ID and MT
Seattle WA 98174-1067	
Phone: (206) 220-7037	
Fax: (206) 220-7245	
E-mail: D13N11	
CDR, 14th CG Dist. (b)	
300 Ala Moana Blvd.	Hawaii and U.S. Pacific
Honolulu HI 96850-4982	islands west of longitude
Phone: (808) 541-2121	150W and south of latitude
Fax: (808) 541-2175	40N
E-mail: DPA1/D14	
CDR, 17th CG Dist. (ba)	
P.O. Box 25517	Alaska
Juno, AK 99802-5517	
Phone: (907) 463-2065	
Fax: (907) 463-2072	
E-mail: R. Massey/D17-10	

APPENDIX E

STATE BOATING LAW ADMINISTRATORS

(Alphabetical by State)

Director, Marine Police Division
Department of Conservation and Natural
    Resources
674 North Union Street, Room 756
Montgomery, Alabama 36130
Tel. (205) 242-3673-3676
Fax. (205) 240-3336

Assistant Commander
Department of Public Safety
Pago Pago, American Samoa 96799
Tel. (684) 633-1111
Fax. (684) 633-7035

State Boating Administrator
Arizona Game and Fish Department
2222 West Greenway Road
Phoenix, Arizona 85023
Tel. (602) 942-3000/ext. 491
Fax. (602) 789-3920/1

Boating Safety Program Administrator
Arkansas Game and Fish Commission
#2 Natural Resources Drive
Little Rock, Arkansas 72205
Tel. (501) 223-6399
Fax. (501) 223-6447

Director
Department of Boating and Waterways
1629 S Street
Sacramento, California 95814
Tel. (916) 445-9657
Fax. (916) 327-7250

Boating Administrator
Division of Parks and Outdoor Recreation
13787 South Highway 80
Littleton, Colorado 80125
Tel. (303) 791-1954
Fax. (303) 470-0782

Boating Law Administrator
DEP Complex
PO Box 271
163 Great Hill Road
Portland, Connecticut 06480
Tel. (203) 344-2668
Fax. (203) 344-2560

Boating Law Administrator
Division of Fish and Wildlife
Richardson & Robbins Building
PO Box 1401
Dover, Delaware 19903
Tel. (302) 739-3440
Fax. (302) 739-3491

Metropolitan Police Department
MPDC Harbor Branch
550 Water Street, SW
Washington, DC 20024
Tel. (202) 727-4582
Fax. (202) 727-3663

Boating Law Administrator
Florida Marine Patrol
3900 Commonwealth Boulevard
Tallahassee, Florida 32399-3000
Tel. (904) 488-5757
Fax. (904) 488-6425

Department of Natural Resources
Assistant Chief, Law Enforcement
2109-A U.S. Highway 278, S.E.
Social Circle, Georgia 30279
Tel. (404) 656-3534/3510
Fax. (404) 656-4992

Boating Law Administrator
Guam Police Department
Special Programs Section
287 West O'Brien Drive
Agana, Guam 96910
Tel. (671) 472-8911
Fax. (671) 472-9704

State Boating Manager
Department of Transportation
79 South Nimitz Highway
Honolulu, Hawaii 96813
Tel. (808) 548-2838/2515
Fax. (808) 587-1977

Boating Program Supervisor
Department of Parks and Recreation
PO Box 83720
Boise, Idaho 83720-0065
Tel. (208) 334-4199
Fax. (208) 334-3741

Boating Law Administrator
Division of Law Enforcement
Department of Conservation
524 South Second Street
Springfield, Illinois 62701-1787
Tel. (217) 782-6431
Fax. (217) 785-8405

State Boating Law Administrator
Department of Natural Resources
402 W Washington Street, Room W-255D
Indianapolis, Indiana 46204
Tel. (317) 232-4010
Fax. (317) 232-8035

Director, Department of Natural Resources
Wallace Building
Des Moines, Iowa 50319-0035
Tel. (515) 281-8688
Fax. (515) 281-8895

Boating Administrator
Kansas Wildlife and Parks
RR2, Box 54A
Pratt, Kansas 67124
Tel. (316) 672-5911/ext. 158
Fax. (316) 672-6020

Director, Kentucky Water Patrol
Department of Natural Resources
107 Mero Street
Frankfort, Kentucky 40601
Tel. (502) 564-3074
Fax. (502) 564-6193

Boating Law Administrator
Department of Wildlife and Fisheries
PO Box 98000
Baton Rouge, Louisiana 70898-9000
Tel. (504) 765-2988
Fax. (504) 765-2832

Inland Fisheries and Wildlife
284 State Street, Station #41
Augusta, Maine 04333
Tel. (207) 289-2766
Fax. (207) 289-6395

Maryland Department of Natural Resources
Tawes State Office Building
580 Taylor Avenue
Annapolis, Maryland 21401
Tel. (301) 974-3548
Fax. (301) 974-2740

Director
Division of Law Enforcement
100 Nashua Street
Boston, Massachusetts 02114
Tel. (617) 727-3905
Fax. (617) 727-2754

Chief, Law Enforcement Division
Department of Natural Resources
PO Box 30028
Lansing, Michigan 48909
Tel. (517) 373-1230
Fax. (517) 373-6816

Boat and Water Safety Coordinator
Department of Natural Resources
Box 46, 500 Lafayette Road
St. Paul, Minnesota 55155-4046
Tel. (612) 296-3310
Fax. (612) 296-0902

Boating Law Administrator
Department of Wildlife, Fisheries and Parks
PO Box 451
Jackson, Mississippi 39205
Tel. (601) 364-2187
Fax. (601) 364-2125

Commissioner, Missouri State Water Patrol
Department of Public Safety
PO Box 1368
Jefferson City, Missouri 65102-1368
Tel. (314) 751-3333
Fax. (314) 636-8428

Boating Law Administrator
Boating Safety Division
Department of Fish, Wildlife and Parks
1420 East 6th Avenue
Helena, Montana 59620
Tel. (406) 444-2452
Fax. (406) 444-4952

Boating Law Administrator
Game and Parks Commission
PO Box 30370
Lincoln, Nebraska 68503-0370
Tel. (402) 471-5579
Fax. (402) 471-5528

Chief, Division of Law Enforcement
Department of Wildlife
PO Box 10678
Reno, Nevada 89520-0022
Tel. (702) 688-1500
Fax. (702) 688-1595

Director of Administration
New Hampshire Department of Safety
Hazen Drive
Concord, New Hampshire 03305
Tel. (603) 271-2589
Fax. (603) 271-3903

Boating Law Administrator
New Jersey State Police
Marine Law Enforcement Bureau
PO Box 7068
West Trenton, New Jersey 08628-0068
Tel. (609) 882-2000/ext. 2530/2531
Fax. (609) 882-6523

Boating Administrator
Energy, Minerals and Natural Resources
    Department
Parks and Recreation Division
PO Box 1147
Santa Fe, New Mexico 87504-1147
Tel. (505) 827-3986
Fax. (505) 827-4001

Director, Bureau of Marine and Recreational
    Vehicles
Agency Building #1, 13th Floor
Empire State Plaza
Albany, New York 12238
Tel. (518) 474-0445
Fax. (518) 474-4492

Executive Director
Wildlife Resource Commission
512 North Salisbury Street
Archdale Building
Raleigh, North Carolina 27604-1188
Tel. (919) 733-3391
Fax. (919) 733-7083

Boat and Water Safety Coordinator
State Game and Fish Department
100 North Bismarck Expressway
Bismarck, North Dakota 58501 5095
Tel. (701) 221-6300
Fax. (701) 221-6832

Chief, Division of Watercraft
Department of Natural Resources
Fountain Square, C-2
Columbus, Ohio 43224
Tel. (614) 265-6480
Fax. (614) 267-8883

Director, Lake Patrol Division
Department of Public Safety
PO Box 11415
Oklahoma City, Oklahoma 73136-0415
Tel. (405) 425-2143
Fax. (405) 425-2268

Director
State Marine Board
435 Commercial Street, N.E.
Salem, Oregon 97310
Tel. (503) 378-8587
Fax. (503) 378-4597

Director, Bureau of Boating
Pennsylvania Fish and Boat Commission
PO Box 1673
Harrisburg, Pennsylvania 17105-1673
Tel. (717) 657-4538
Fax. (717) 657-4549

Commissioner of Navigation
Department of Natural Resources
PO Box 5887
Puerta de Tierra, Puerto Rico 00906
Tel. (809) 724-2340
Fax. (809) 724-7335

Division of Enforcement
Department of Environmental Management
83 Park Street
Providence, Rhode Island 02903-1037
Tel. (401) 277-3070
Fax. (401) 277-6823

Boating Law Administrator
Wildlife and Marine Resources Department
PO Box 12559
Charleston, South Carolina 29412
Tel. (803) 762-5041
Fax. (803) 762-5007/5001

Boating Safety Coordinator
Department of Game, Fish and Parks
Anderson Building, 445 East Capitol
Pierre, South Dakota 57501
Tel. (605) 773-4506
Fax. (605) 773-6245

Supervisor, Water Safety Law Enforcement
Texas Parks and Wildlife Department
4200 Smith School Road
Austin, Texas 78744
Tel. (512) 389-4850
Fax. (512) 389-4740

Boating Law Administrator
Tennessee Wildlife Resources Agency
PO Box 40747
Nashville, Tennessee 37204-9979
Tel. (615) 781-6682
Fax. (615) 741-4606

Boating Law Administrator
Division of Parks and Recreation
1636 West North Temple Street
Salt Lake City, Utah 84116
Tel. (801) 538-7341
Fax. (801) 538-7315

Boating Law Administrator
Vermont State Police Headquarters
103 South Main Street
Waterbury, Vermont 05676
Tel. (802) 244-8778
Fax. (802) 244-1106

Boating Law Administrator
Department of Planning and Natural Re-
    sources
Nisky Center, Suite 231
St. Thomas, Virgin Islands 00802
Tel. (809) 774-3320
Fax. (809) 775-5706

Boating Law Administrator
Department of Game and Inland Fisheries
PO Box 11104
Richmond, Virginia 23230-1104
Tel. (804) 367-1189
Fax. (804) 367-9147

Boating Safety Administrator
Washington State Parks and Recreation
    Commission
7150 Cleanwater Lane (KY-11)
Olympia, Washington 98504
Tel. (206) 586-2165
Fax. (206) 753-1594

Chief, Law Enforcement Section
Division of Natural Resources
Capitol Complex Boulevard East
1900 Kanawha Boulevard East
Charleston, West Virginia 25305
Tel. (304) 558-2784
Fax. (304) 348-2768

Boating Law Administrator
Department of Natural Resources
PO Box 7924
Madison, Wisconsin 53707
Tel. (608) 266-0859
Fax. (608) 267-3579/266-3696

Wildlife Law Enforcement Coordinator
Game and Fish Department
5400 Bishop Boulevard
Cheyenne, Wyoming 82006
Tel. (307) 777-4579
Fax. (307) 777-4610

Director
Department of Public Safety
Civic Center
Saipan, CNMI 96950
Tel. (670) 234-6021/606
Fax. (670) 234-2023

APPENDIX F

ACCIDENT REPORT FORM

DEPARTMENT OF TRANSPORTATION U.S. COAST GUARD CG-3865(REV. X/94)	BOATING ACCIDENT REPORT

State Assigned Case No. _____

FORM APPROVED
OMB NO. 2115-0010

The operator/owner of a vessel used for recreational purposes is required to file a report in writing whenever an accident results in: loss of life or disappearance from a vessel; an injury that requires medical treatment beyond first aid; or property damage in excess of $500 or complete loss of the vessel. Reports in death and injury cases must be submitted within 48 hours. Reports in other cases must be submitted within 10 days. Reports must be submitted to the reporting authority in the state where the accident occurred. This form is provided to assist the operator in filing the required written report.

COMPLETE ALL BLOCKS (indicate those not applicable by "N/A")

ACCIDENT DATA

DATE OF ACCIDENT	TIME am pm	NAME OF BODY OF WATER	LOCATION (Give location precisely)		
NUMBER OF VESSELS INVOLVED	NEAREST CITY OR TOWN	COUNTY		STATE	ZIP CODE

WEATHER (check all that apply)	WATER CONDITIONS	TEMPERATURE (estimate)	WIND	VISIBILITY
[ ] Clear [ ] Rain [ ] Cloudy [ ] Snow [ ] Fog [ ] Hazy	[ ] Calm (waves less than 6") [ ] Choppy (waves 6" - 2') [ ] Rough (waves 2' - 6') [ ] Very Rough (greater than 6') [ ] Strong Current	Air _____ °F Water _____ °F	[ ] None [ ] Light (0-6 mph) [ ] Moderate (7-14 mph) [ ] Strong (15-25 mph) [ ] Storm (over 25 mph)	Day Night [ ] Good [ ] [ ] Fair [ ] [ ] Poor [ ]

NAME OF OPERATOR	OPERATOR ADDRESS		
OPERATOR TELEPHONE NUMBER ( ) [ ] Male [ ] Female	DATE OF BIRTH mo day yr	OPERATOR'S EXPERIENCE [ ] Under 10 hours [ ] 10 - 100 hours [ ] Over 100 hours	FORMAL INSTRUCTION IN BOATING SAFETY [ ] State Course [ ] U.S. Power Squadron [ ] USCG Auxiliary [ ] American Red Cross [ ] Informal [ ] None
NAME OF OWNER	OWNER ADDRESS		

OWNER TELEPHONE NUMBER ( )	NUMBER OF People on Board	NUMBER OF People Being Towed	RENTED BOAT? [ ] Yes [ ] No

BOAT NO. 1 (This vessel)

BOAT REGISTRATION OR DOCUMENTATION NUMBER	STATE	HULL IDENIFICATION NUMBER	BOAT NAME
BOAT MANUFACTURER	MODEL	LENGTH	YEAR BUILT

TYPE OF BOAT	HULL MATERIAL	ENGINE	PROPULSION	PERSONAL FLOTATION DEVICES (PFDs)
[ ] Open Motorboat [ ] Cabin Motorboat [ ] Auxiliary Sail [ ] Sail (only) [ ] Rowboat [ ] Canoe/Kayak [ ] Personal Watercraft [ ] Pontoon Boat [ ] Houseboat [ ] Other (specify)	[ ] Wood [ ] Aluminum [ ] Steel [ ] Fiberglass [ ] Rubber/vinyl/canvas [ ] Rigid Hull Inflatable [ ] Other (specify)	[ ] Outboard [ ] Inboard [ ] Inboard- Sterndrive (I/O) [ ] Airboat FUEL [ ] Gasoline [ ] Diesel [ ] Electric	[ ] Propeller [ ] Water Jet [ ] Air Thrust [ ] Manual [ ] Sail NO. OF ENGINES TOTAL HORSEPOWER	Was the boat adequately equipped with COAST GUARD APPROVED PFDs? [ ] Yes [ ] No Were PFDs accessible? [ ] Yes [ ] No FIRE EXTINGUISHERS On Board [ ] Yes [ ] No Used [ ] Yes [ ] No [ ] N/A

OPERATION AT TIME OF ACCIDENT (check all applicable)	ACTIVITY AT TIME OF ACCIDENT (check all applicable)	TYPE OF ACCIDENT	WHAT CONTRIBUTED TO ACCIDENT (check all applicable)
[ ] Cruising [ ] Changing Direction [ ] Changing Speed [ ] Drifting [ ] Towing [ ] Being Towed [ ] Rowing/Paddling [ ] Sailing [ ] Launching [ ] Docking/Undocking [ ] At Anchor [ ] Tied to Dock/Moored [ ] Other (specify)	[ ] Fishing [ ] Tournament [ ] Hunting [ ] Swimming/Diving [ ] Making Repairs [ ] Waterskiing/Tubing/Etc. [ ] Racing [ ] Whitewater Sports [ ] Fueling [ ] Non-Recreational [ ] Other (specify)	[ ] Grounding [ ] Capsizing [ ] Flooding/Swamping [ ] Sinking [ ] Fire or Explosion (Fuel) [ ] Fire or Explosion (Other than Fuel) [ ] Skier Mishap [ ] Collision with Vessel [ ] Collision with Fixed Object [ ] Collision with Floating Object [ ] Falls Overboard [ ] Falls in Boat [ ] Struck by Boat [ ] Struck by Motor/Propeller [ ] Other [ ] Hit and Run	[ ] Weather [ ] Excessive Speed [ ] No Skier Lookout [ ] Restricted Vision [ ] Overloading [ ] Improper Loading [ ] Hazardous Waters [ ] Alcohol Use [ ] Drug Use [ ] Hull Failure [ ] Machinery Failure [ ] Equipment Failure [ ] Operator Inexperience [ ] Operator Inattention [ ] Congested Waters [ ] Passenger/Skier Behavior [ ] Dam/Lock [ ] Other (specify)
ESTIMATED SPEED [ ] Under 10 mph [ ] 10 - 20 mph [ ] Over 20 mph [ ] Over 40 mph			

DECEASED (If more than 2 fatalities, attach additional forms)

NAME OF VICTIM	ADDRESS OF VICTIM		
DATE OF BIRTH [ ] Male [ ] Female	DEATH CAUSED BY [ ] Drowning [ ] Other		[ ] Disappearance
	WAS PFD WORN? [ ] Yes [ ] No		
NAME OF VICTIM	ADDRESS OF VICTIM		
DATE OF BIRTH [ ] Male [ ] Female	DEATH CAUSED BY [ ] Drowning [ ] Other		[ ] Disappearance
	WAS PFD WORN? [ ] Yes [ ] No		

INJURED (If more than 2 injuries, attach additional form)

NAME OF VICTIM	ADDRESS OF VICTIM			
DATE OF BIRTH	MEDICAL TREATMENT BEYOND FIRST AID?		[ ] Yes	[ ] No
	ADMITTED TO HOSPITAL?		[ ] Yes	[ ] No
	DESCRIBE INJURY			
	WAS PFD WORN? [ ] Yes [ ] No	PRIOR TO ACCIDENT?	[ ] Yes	[ ] No
	WAS IT INFLATABLE? [ ] Yes [ ] No	AS A RESULT OF ACCIDENT?	[ ] Yes	[ ] No
NAME OF VICTIM	ADDRESS OF VICTIM			
DATE OF BIRTH	MEDICAL TREATMENT BEYOND FIRST AID?		[ ] Yes	[ ] No
	ADMITTED TO HOSPITAL?		[ ] Yes	[ ] No
	DESCRIBE INJURY			
	WAS PFD WORN? [ ] Yes [ ] No	PRIOR TO ACCIDENT?	[ ] Yes	[ ] No
	WAS IT INFLATABLE? [ ] Yes [ ] No	AS A RESULT OF ACCIDENT?	[ ] Yes	[ ] No

OTHER PEOPLE ABOARD THIS BOAT (If more than 2 people, attach additional form)

NAME	ADDRESS			
DATE OF BIRTH	WAS PFD WORN? [ ] Yes [ ] No	PRIOR TO ACCIDENT?	[ ] Yes	[ ] No
	WAS IT INFLATABLE? [ ] Yes [ ] No	AS A RESULT OF ACCIDENT?	[ ] Yes	[ ] No
NAME	ADDRESS			
DATE OF BIRTH	WAS PFD WORN? [ ] Yes [ ] No	PRIOR TO ACCIDENT?	[ ] Yes	[ ] No
	WAS IT INFLATABLE? [ ] Yes [ ] No	AS A RESULT OF ACCIDENT?	[ ] Yes	[ ] No

VESSEL NO. 2 (If more than 2 vessels, attach additional form)

NAME OF OPERATOR	OPERATOR ADDRESS	
OPERATOR TELEPHONE NUMBER	BOAT REGISTRATION OR DOCUMENTATION NUMBER	STATE
NAME OF OPERATOR	OPERATOR ADDRESS	
OPERATOR TELEPHONE NUMBER	BOAT REGISTRATION OR DOCUMENTATION NUMBER	STATE

PROPERTY DAMAGE

NAME OF OWNER OF DAMAGED PROPERTY OTHER THAN VESSELS	ADDRESS
ESTIMATED AMOUNT THIS BOAT $ OTHER BOAT(s) $ OTHER PROPERTY $	DESCRIBE PROPERTY DAMAGE

app•F2

ACCIDENT DESCRIPTION

DESCRIBE WHAT HAPPENED (Sequence of events. Include Failure of Equipment. If diagram needed, attach seperately. Continue on additional sheets if necessary. Include any information regarding the involvement of alcohol and/or drugs in causing or contributing to the accident. Including any descriptive information about the use of PFDs.)

WITNESSES NOT ON THIS VESSEL

NAME	ADDRESS	TELEPHONE NUMBER ( )
NAME	ADDRESS	TELEPHONE NUMBER ( )
NAME	ADDRESS	TELEPHONE NUMBER ( )

PERSON COMPLETING REPORT

NAME	ADDRESS	TELEPHONE NUMBER ( )
SIGNATURE	QUALIFICATION [ ] Operator [ ] Owner [ ] Investigator [ ] Other	DATE SUBMITTED

(Do not use) FOR REPORTING AUTHORITY REVIEW (Use agency date stamp)

Causes based on (check one) [ ] This report [ ] Investigation and this report [ ] Investigation [ ] Could not be determined	Name of Reviewing Officer	Date Received

app•F3

FLOAT PLAN

Complete this plan, before going boating and leave it with a reliable person who can be depended upon to notify the Coast Guard, or other rescue organization, should you not return as scheduled. Do not file this plan with the Coast Guard.

TODAY'S DATE _____ (if overnight, date returning) _____

1. NAME OF PERSON REPORTING _____

TELEPHONE NUMBER _____

2. DESCRIPTION OF BOAT. TYPE _____

COLOR _____ TRIM _____

REGISTRATION NO. _____ LENGTH _____

NAME _____ MAKE _____

OTHER INFO. _____

3. NUMBER OF PERSONS ABOARD _____

NAME _____ NAME _____

AGE _____ AGE _____

ADDRESS _____ ADDRESS _____

_____ - _____

PHONE # _____ PHONE # _____

Please list additional passengers and information on the back of this form.

4. TRIP EXPECTATIONS: LEAVE AT _____ (TIME)

FROM _____

GOING TO _____

EXPECT TO RETURN BY _____ (TIME)

AND IN NO EVENT LATER THAN _____ (TIME)

5. IF NOT RETURNED BY _____ (TIME) CALL THE COAST GUARD, OR

_____ (LOCAL AUTHORITY)

TELEPHONE NUMBERS _____

6. ENGINE TYPE _____ H.P. _____

NO. OF ENGINES _____ FUEL CAPACITY _____

7. SURVIVAL EQUIPMENT: (CHECK AS APPROPRIATE)

☐ PFDs   ☐ FLARES   ☐ MIRROR   ☐ SMOKE SIGNALS

☐ CLOTHING   ☐ FLASHLIGHT   ☐ FOOD   ☐ PADDLES

☐ WATER   ☐ OTHERS   ☐ ANCHOR   ☐ RAFT OR DINGHY

☐ EPIRB

8. RADIO: ☐ YES ☐ NO

TYPE _____ FREQS. _____

9. ANY OTHER PERTINENT INFO. _____

_____

10. AUTOMOBILE LICENSE _____ TYPE _____

TRAILER LICENSE _____ COLOR AND MAKE OF AUTO _____

WHERE PARKED _____

MAKE ADDITIONAL COPIES OF THIS FORM FOR YOUR USE

APPENDIX H

END OF COURSE EXAMINATION

Directions: Select the choice that best answers the question or completes the statement. Using a number 2 pencil, completely fill in the circle on the answer sheet that matches your answer.

1. A reliable indicator of how many people a boat can safely carry is the
   A. number of seats in the boat
   B. salesperson's recommendation
   C. manufacturer's capacity plate
   D. the overall length of the boat

2. Federal law regarding Personal Flotation Devices (PFDs) states that they
   A. should be stored in sealed bags
   B. must be Coast Guard Approved
   C. can be any size
   D. must be international orange in color

3. The type of PFD used to turn nearly all persons face up is
   A. Type I
   B. Type III
   C. Type IV
   D. Type II

4. Coast Guard-approved fire extinguishers are classified by
   A. Underwriter's Laboratories (UL)
   B. the types of fire they extinguish
   C. length of boat they are used on
   D. overall weight of unit

5. Visual Distress Signals (VDSs) are required for daylight operation on
   A. manually propelled boats
   B. recreational boats less than 16 feet
   C. Boats participating in organized races
   D. sailboats 16 feet or over with auxiliary motors

6. VDSs which meet the requirements for day and night use are
   A. hand held flares
   B. orange smoke signals
   C. electric distress lights
   D. orange flag with black ball over black square

7. The greatest cause of fire and explosions on board recreational boats is
   A. gasoline vapor in bilge
   B. smoking while fueling gas tank
   C. not venting the gasoline tank properly
   D. galley stoves

8. Boats at least 26 feet operating on federal waters must display a
   A. marine sanitation placard
   B. discharge of oil placard
   C. waste management placard
   D. Coast Guard Auxiliary CME decal

9. When caught out in foul weather, the first thing to do is
   A. use the distress signal
   B. drop the anchor
   C. head for shelter
   D. call USCG on Marine Radio Channel 16

10. At the end of the boat trip, remember to
    A. refuel the gas tank
    B. cancel the float plan
    C. check fire extinguishers
    D. change oil and all hydraulic fluids

11. There are several different Navigation Lights, one is the sidelight. The color of a sidelight is
    A. green
    B. white
    C. yellow
    D. amber

12. The responsibility for preventing accidents rests with
    A. the give way boat only
    B. the stand on boat only
    C. both boats
    D. boat approaching from upwind

13. A red rectangular flag with a single white diagonal stripe means
    A. vessels engaging in diving operations
    B. areas reserved for swimmers
    C. there are divers present
    D. no wake zone, proceed at idle speed

14. The color of a NUN buoy is
    A. red
    B. green
    C. orange
    D. black

15. Aids to Navigation (AtoN) are provided to help the boater
    A. tie up to them
    B. treat them with respect
    C. anchor close to them
    D. ignore them if in a boat 16 feet or less

16. The red and white vertically striped buoy in th U.S.W.M.S. means
    A. an obstruction exists between the buoy and the shore
    B. an obstruction exists and pass buoy South or West
    C. an obstruction exists and pass buoy North or East
    D. an obstruction exists between the next series of buoys

17. A magnetic compass shows
    A. variation in areas
    B. locations of AtoNs
    C. magnetic North
    D. deviation of 3 degrees

18. A good approach angle when docking is
    A. 10 degrees
    B. 20 degrees
    C. 30 degrees
    D. 90 degrees

19. The most dangerous way to anchor a boat is to:
    A. lower the anchor hand over hand
    B. attach the anchor line to the stern of the boat
    C. use an anchor line about 7 times the water depth
    D. attach a tripline when over a rocky bottom

20. What action should a skipper take when retrieving a person who has fallen
    overboard?
    A. speed up the engine to get the person
    B. maneuver boat downwind of person
    C. have someone serve as spotter
    D. retrieve person in water over the bow

21. To avoid falls overboard
    A. sit on gunwhale
    B. keep low in boat
    C. drink alcoholic beverages
    D. position all passengers toward the stern of the boat

22. One tip to remember when waterskiing is
    A. that the waterskier may wear any type of PFD
    B. it is good to ski in rough water
    C. to have an observer in the tow boat
    D. the boat towing the skier always has the right-of-way on the water

23. The maximum legal width of a trailer and boat without permit is
    A. 8$\frac{1}{2}$ feet
    B. 10 feet
    C. 12 feet
    D. 6 feet

24. For the courtesy of others, prepare the boat for launching by
    A. releasing winch line from bow
    B. starting the boat motor
    C. removing the transom drain plug
    D. readying the boat for launch in the parking lot prior to proceeding to the ramp

25. A responsible boat operator consumes
    A. alcohol when operating a vessel alone
    B. an amount of alcohol he/she knows can be handled
    C. alcohol only when operating a boat on calm water
    D. no alcoholic beverages prior to, or when operating a boat

APPENDIX I

END OF COURSE EXAMINATION ANSWER SHEET

The answer sheet provided on the next page is used to support several courses. For <u>this</u> course, use only answer blocks <u>1 through 25.</u>

To receive your "Skipper's Course" certificate, complete the End of Course Exam and mail to:
United States Coast Guard Auxiliary
9449 Watson Industrial Park
St. Louis, Mo 63126

Your Name: _____	**Telephone:** _____ *(Optional)*
Street Address: _____	**Region:** _____
City and State: _____	**Zip Code:** _____

ANSWER SHEET FOR SKIPPER'S COURSE TEST

DIRECTIONS: Completely black out the ovals under the letter corresponding to your choice with pen or pencil, like this: ●;

NOT THIS: ☑ ☒ ◯ When you are finished, please remove this page, fold, tape, and mail it to the designated location.

	A	B	C	D		A	B	C	D		A	B	C	D
1.	◯	◯	◯	◯	18.	◯	◯	◯	◯	35.	◯	◯	◯	◯
2.	◯	◯	◯	◯	19.	◯	◯	◯	◯	36.	◯	◯	◯	◯
3.	◯	◯	◯	◯	20.	◯	◯	◯	◯	37.	◯	◯	◯	◯
4.	◯	◯	◯	◯	21.	◯	◯	◯	◯	38.	◯	◯	◯	◯
5.	◯	◯	◯	◯	22.	◯	◯	◯	◯	39.	◯	◯	◯	◯
6.	◯	◯	◯	◯	23.	◯	◯	◯	◯	40.	◯	◯	◯	◯
7.	◯	◯	◯	◯	24.	◯	◯	◯	◯	41.	◯	◯	◯	◯
8.	◯	◯	◯	◯	25.	◯	◯	◯	◯	42.	◯	◯	◯	◯
9.	◯	◯	◯	◯	26.	◯	◯	◯	◯	43.	◯	◯	◯	◯
10.	◯	◯	◯	◯	27.	◯	◯	◯	◯	44.	◯	◯	◯	◯
11.	◯	◯	◯	◯	28.	◯	◯	◯	◯	45.	◯	◯	◯	◯
12.	◯	◯	◯	◯	29.	◯	◯	◯	◯	46.	◯	◯	◯	◯
13.	◯	◯	◯	◯	30.	◯	◯	◯	◯	47.	◯	◯	◯	◯
14.	◯	◯	◯	◯	31.	◯	◯	◯	◯	48.	◯	◯	◯	◯
15.	◯	◯	◯	◯	32.	◯	◯	◯	◯	49.	◯	◯	◯	◯
16.	◯	◯	◯	◯	33.	◯	◯	◯	◯	50.	◯	◯	◯	◯
17.	◯	◯	◯	◯	34.	◯	◯	◯	◯					

The following optional information will enable the USCG and Coast Guard Auxiliary to provide a quality boating safety education program.

	M	F		12–16	17–25	26–50	Over 50
SEX:	◯	◯	**AGE GROUP:**	◯	◯	◯	◯

PRIMARY OPERATING CRAFT:

	less than <16'	16'–25'	26'–39'	40'–65'
POWER:	◯	◯	◯	◯
SAIL:	◯	◯	◯	◯

OTHER: _____ **Length of Craft** _____

	Inland	Coastal	Lakes	Other
OPERATING WATERWAY: *(Mark all that apply.)*	◯	◯	◯	◯

FOR OFFICE USE ONLY. *(Do not write in this box.)*

		0	1	2	3	4	5	6	7	8	9
	STUDENT ID: _____	◯	◯	◯	◯	◯	◯	◯	◯	◯	◯
DATE: _____	_____	◯	◯	◯	◯	◯	◯	◯	◯	◯	◯
	_____	◯	◯	◯	◯	◯	◯	◯	◯	◯	◯

GLOSSARY OF TERMS

A

ABAFT - Toward the rear (stern) of the boat. Behind.

ABEAM - At right angles to the keel of the boat, but not on the boat.

ABOARD - On or within the boat.

ABOVE DECK - On the deck (not over it — see ALOFT).

AFT - Toward the stern of the boat.

AGROUND - Touching or fast to the bottom.

AHEAD - In a forward direction.

AIDS TO NAVIGATION (AtoN) - Artificial objects to supplement natural landmarks to indicate safe and unsafe waters.

ALOFT - Above the deck of the boat.

AMIDSHIPS - In or toward the center of the boat.

ANCHOR - A heavy metal device, fastened to chain or line, to hold a vessel in position, partly because of its weight, but chiefly because the designed shape digs into the bottom.

ANCHORAGE - A place suitable for anchoring in relation to the wind, seas and bottom.

ASTERN - In back of the boat, opposite of ahead.

ATHWARTSHIPS - At right angles to the centerline of the boat; rowboat seats are generally athwartships.

B

BATTEN DOWN - Secure hatches and loose objects both within the hull and on deck.

BEACON - A lighted or unlighted fixed aid to navigation attached directly to the earth's surface. (Lights and daybeacons both constitute "beacons.")

BEAM - The greatest width of the boat.

BEARING - The direction of an object expressed either as a true bearing as shown on the chart, or as a bearing relative to the heading of the boat.

BELOW - Beneath the deck.

BIGHT - The part of the rope or line, between the end and the standing part, on which a knot is formed. A shallow bay.

BILGE - The interior of the hull below the floor boards.

BITTER END - The last part of a rope or chain. The inboard end of the anchor rode.

BLOCK - A wooden or metal case enclosing one or more pulleys and having a hook, eye, or strap by which it may be attached.

BOAT - A fairly indefinite term. A waterborne vehicle smaller than a ship. One definition is a small craft carried aboard a ship.

BOAT HOOK - A short shaft with a fitting at one end shaped to facilitate use in putting a line over a piling, recovering an object dropped overboard, or in pushing or fending off.

BOW - The forward part of a boat.

BOW LINE - A docking line leading from the bow.

BOW SPRING LINE - A bow pivot line used in docking and undocking, or to prevent the boat from moving forward or astern while made fast to a picr.

BOWLINE - A knot used to form a temporary loop in the end of a line.

BOWSPRIT - A spar extending forward from the bow.

BRIDGE - The location from which a vessel is steered and its speed controlled. "Control Station" is really a more appropriate term for small craft.

BULKHEAD - A vertical partition separating compartments.

BUOY - An anchored float used for marking a position on the water or a hazard or a shoal and for mooring.

C

CABIN - A compartment for passengers or crew.

CAPSIZE - To turn over.

CAST OFF - To let go.

CATAMARAN - A twin-hulled boat, with hulls side by side.

CHAFING GEAR - Tubing or cloth wrapping used to protect a line from chafing on a rough surface.

CHANNEL - 1. That part of a body of water deep enough for navigation through an area otherwise not suitable. It is usually marked by a single or double line of buoys and sometimes by range markers. 2. The deepest part of a stream, bay, or strait, through which the main current flows. 3. A name given to a large strait, for example, the English Channel.

CHART - A map for use by navigators.

CHINE - The intersection of the bottom and sides of a flat or v-bottomed boat.

CHOCK - A fitting through which anchor or mooring lines are led. Usually U-shaped to reduce chafe.

CLEAT - A fitting to which lines are made fast. The classic cleat to which lines are belayed is approximately anvil-shaped.

CLOVE HITCH - A knot for temporarily fastening a line to a spar or piling.

COAMING - A vertical piece around the edge of a cockpit, hatch, etc. to prevent water on deck from running below.

COCKPIT - An opening in the deck from which the boat is handled.

COIL - To lay a line down in circular turns.

COMPASS - Navigation instrument, either magnetic (showing magnetic north) or gyro (showing true north).

COMPASS CARD - Part of a compass, the card is graduated in degrees, to conform with the magnetic meridian-referenced direction system inscribed with direction which remains constant; the vessel turns, not the card.

COMPASS ROSE - The resulting figure when the complete 360° directional system is developed as a circle with each degree graduated upon it, and with the 000° indicated as True North. Also called true rose. This is printed on nautical charts for determining direction.

CURRENT - The horizontal movement of water.

D

DAYBEACON - A fixed navigation aid structure used in shallow waters upon which is placed one or more Daymarks.

DAYMARK - A signboard attached to a daybeacon to convey navigational information presenting one of several standard shapes (square, triangle, rectangle, diamond, octagon) and colors (red, green, orange, yellow, or black). Daymarks usually have reflective material indicating the shape, but may also be lighted.

DEAD AHEAD - Directly ahead.

DEAD ASTERN - Directly aft or behind.

DEAD RECKONING - A plot of courses steered and distances traveled through the water.

DECK - A permanent covering over a compartment, hull or any part of a ship serving as a floor.

DISPLACEMENT - The weight of water displaced by a floating vessel.

DISPLACEMENT HULL - A type of hull that plows through the water, displacing a weight of water equal to its own weight, even when more power is added.

DOCK - A protected water area in which vessels are moored. The term is often used to denote a pier or a wharf.

DRAFT - The depth of water a boat draws.

E

EASE - To slacken or relieve tension on a line.

EBB TIDE - A receding tide.

EVEN KEEL - When a boat is floating on its designed waterline, it is said to be floating on an even keel.

EYE OF THE WIND - The direction from which the wind is blowing.

EYE SPLICE - A permanent loop spliced in the end of a line.

F

FAST - Said of an object that is secured to another.

FATHOM - Six feet.

FENDER - A cushion, placed between boats, or between a boat and a pier, to prevent damage.

FIGURE EIGHT KNOT - A knot in the form of a figure eight, placed in the end of a line to prevent the line from passing through a grommet or a block.

FLAME ARRESTER - A safety device, such as a metal mesh protector, to prevent an exhaust backfire from causing an explosion; operates by absorbing heat.

FLARE - The outward curve of a vessel's sides near the bow. A distress signal.

FLYING BRIDGE - An added set of controls above the level of the normal control station for better visibility. Usually open, but may have a collapsible top for shade.

FOLLOWING SEA - A sea that comes from astern.

FORE AND AFT - In a line parallel to the keel.

FORWARD - Toward the bow of the boat.

FOULED - Any piece of equipment that is jammed or entangled, or dirtied.

FOUNDER - When a vessel fills with water and sinks.

FREEBOARD - The minimum vertical distance from the surface of the water to the gunwale.

G

GAFF - A spar to support the head of a gaff sail.

GALLEY - The kitchen area of a boat.

GANGWAY - The area of a ship's side where people board and disembark.

GEAR - A general term for ropes, blocks, tackle and other equipment.

GIVE-WAY VESSEL - A term, from the Navigational Rules, used to describe the vessel which must yield in meeting, crossing, or overtaking situations.

GRAB RAILS - Hand-hold fittings mounted on cabin tops and sides for personal safety when moving around the boat.

GROUND TACKLE - Anchor, anchor rode (line or chain), and all the shackles and other gear used for attachment.

GUNWALE - The upper edge of a boat's sides.

H

HARBOR - A safe anchorage, protected from most storms; may be natural or man-made, with breakwaters and jetties; a place for docking and loading.

HATCH - An opening in a boat's deck fitted with a watertight cover.

HEAD - A marine toilet. Also the upper corner of a triangular sail.

HEADING - The direction in which a vessel's bow points at any given time.

HEADWAY - The forward motion of a boat. Opposite of sternway.

HEAVE TO - To bring a vessel up in a position where it will maintain little or no headway, usually with the bow into the wind or nearly so.

HEEL - To tip to one side.

HELM - The wheel or tiller controlling the rudder.

HITCH - A knot used to secure a rope to another object or to another rope, or to form a loop or a noose in a rope.

HOLD - A compartment below deck in a large vessel, used solely for carrying cargo.

HULL - The main body of a vessel.

HYPOTHERMIA - A life-threatening condition in which the body's warming mechanisms fail to maintain normal body temperature and the entire body cools.

I

INBOARD - More toward the center of a vessel; inside; a motor fitted inside the boat.

K

KEDGE - To use an anchor to move a boat by hauling on the anchor rode; a basic anchor type.

KEEL - The centerline of a boat running fore and aft; the backbone of a vessel.

KETCH - a two-masted sailboat with the smaller after mast stepped ahead of the rudder post.

KNOT - A measure of speed equal to one nautical mile (6076 feet) per hour.

KNOT - A fastening made by interweaving rope to form a stopper, to enclose or bind an object, to form a loop or a noose, to tie a small rope to an object, or to tie the ends of two small ropes together.

L

LEEWARD - The direction away from the wind. Opposite of windward.

LEEWAY - The sideways movement of the boat caused by either wind or current.

LINE - Rope and cordage used aboard a vessel.

LOG - A record of courses or operation. Also, a device to measure speed.

LUBBER'S LINE - A mark or permanent line on a compass indicating the direction forward; parallel to the keel when properly installed.

M

MAST - A spar set upright to support rigging and sails.

MONOHULL - A boat with one hull.

MOORING - An arrangement for securing a boat to a mooring buoy or a pier.

MOORING BUOY - A buoy secured to a permanent anchor sunk deeply into the bottom.

N

NAUTICAL MILE - One minute of latitude; approximately 6076 feet - about 1/8 longer than the statute mile of 5280 feet.

NAVIGATION - The art and science of conducting a boat safely from one point to another.

O

OUTBOARD - Toward or beyond the boat's sides. A detachable engine mounted on a boat's stern.

OUTDRIVE - A propulsion system for boats with an inboard engine operating an exterior drive, with driveshaft, gears, and propeller; also called stern-drive and inboard/outboard.

OVERBOARD - Over the side or out of the boat.

P

PAINTER - A line attached to the bow of a boat for use in towing or making fast.

PAY OUT - To ease out a line, or let it run in a controlled manner.

PENNANT (sometimes PENDANT) - The line by which a boat is made fast to a mooring buoy.

PERSONAL FLOTATION DEVICE (PFD) - Official terminology for life jacket. When properly used, will support a person in the water. Available in several sizes and types.

PIER - A loading/landing platform extending at an angle from the shore.

PILOTING - Navigation by use of visible references, the depth of the water, etc.

PITCH - 1. The alternate rise and fall of the bow of a vessel proceeding through waves; 2. The theoretical distance advanced by a propeller in one revolution; 3. Tar and resin used for caulking between the planks of a wooden vessel.

PITCHPOLING - A boat being thrown end-over-end in very rough seas.

PLANING HULL - A type of hull shaped to glide easily across the water at high speed.

PORT - The left side of a boat looking forward. A harbor.

PROPELLER - A rotating device, with two or more blades, that acts as a screw in propelling a vessel.

Q

QUARTER - The sides of a boat aft of amidships.

QUARTERING SEA - Sea coming on a boat's quarter.

R

REEF - To reduce the sail area.

RIGGING - The general term for all the lines of a vessel.

RODE - The anchor line and/or chain.

ROLL - The alternating motion of a boat, leaning alternately to port and starboard; the motion of a boat about its fore-and-aft axis.

ROPE - In general, cordage as it is purchased at the store. When it comes aboard a vessel and is put to use, it becomes a line.

RUDDER - A vertical plate or board for steering a boat.

RUNNING LIGHTS - Lights required to be shown on boats underway between sundown and sunup.

S

SCOPE - The ratio of the length of an anchor line, from a vessel's bow to the anchor, to the depth of the water.

SCREW - A boat's propeller.

SEA ANCHOR - Any device used to reduce a boat's drift before the wind.

SECURE - To make fast.

SHACKLE - A "U" shaped connector with a pin or bolt across the open end.

SHEAR PIN - A safety device, used to fasten a propeller to its shaft; it breaks when the propeller hits a solid object, thus preventing further damage.

SHEET BEND - A knot used to join two ropes. Functionally different from a square knot in that it can be used between lines of different diameters.

SHIP - A larger vessel usually used for ocean travel. A vessel able to carry a "boat" on board.

SHOAL - An offshore hazard to navigation at a depth of 16 fathoms (30 meters) or less, composed of unconsolidated material.

SLACK - Not fastened; loose. Also, to loosen.

SLOOP - A single masted vessel with working sails (main and jib) set fore and aft.

SPLICE - To permanently join two ropes by tucking their strands alternately over and under each other.

SPRING LINE - A pivot line used in docking, undocking, or to prevent the boat from moving forward or astern while made fast to a dock.

SQUALL - A sudden, violent wind often accompanied by rain.

SQUARE KNOT - A knot used to join two lines of similar size. Also called a reef knot.

STANDING PART - That part of a line which is made fast. The main part of a line as distinguished from the bight and the end.

STAND-ON VESSEL - That vessel which continues its course in the same direction at the same speed during a crossing or overtaking situation, unless a collision appears imminent. (Was formerly called "the privileged vessel.")

STARBOARD - The right side of a boat when looking forward.

STERN - The after part (back) of the boat.

STERN LINE - A docking line leading from the stern.

STOW - To pack or store away; especially, to pack in an orderly, compact manner.

SWAMP - To fill with water, but not settle to the bottom.

T

TACKLE - A combination of blocks and line to increase mechanical advantage.

THWART - A seat or brace running laterally across a boat.

TIDE - The periodic rise and fall of water level in the oceans.

TILLER - A bar or handle for turning a boat's rudder or an outboard motor.

TOPSIDES - The sides of a vessel between the waterline and the deck; sometimes referring to onto or above the deck.

TRANSOM - The stern cross-section of a square-sterned boat.

TRIM - Fore and aft balance of a boat.

TRIMARAN - A boat with three hulls.

TRIPLINE - A line fast to the crown of an anchor by means of which it can be hauled out when dug too deeply or fouled; a similar line used on a sea anchor to bring it aboard.

TRUE NORTH POLE - The north end of the earth's axis. Also called North Geographic Pole. The direction indicated by 000° (or 360°) on the true compass rose.

TRUE WIND - The actual direction from which the wind is blowing.

TURNBUCKLE - A threaded, adjustable rigging fitting, used for stays, lifelines and sometimes other rigging.

U

UNDERWAY - Vessel in motion, i.e., when not moored, at anchor, or aground.

V

V BOTTOM - A hull with the bottom section in the shape of a "V."

VARIATION - The angular difference between the magnetic meridian and the geographic meridian at a particular location.

VHF RADIO - A very high frequency electronic communications and direction finding system.

W

WAKE - Moving waves, track or path that a boat leaves behind when moving across the waters.

WATERLINE - A line painted on a hull which shows the point to which a boat sinks when it is properly trimmed.

WAY - Movement of a vessel through the water, such as headway, sternway or leeway.

WHARF - A man-made structure bonding the edge of a dock and built along or at an angle to the shoreline, used for loading, unloading, or tying up vessels.

WINCH - A device used to increase hauling power when raising or trimming sails.

WINDWARD - Toward the direction from which the wind is coming. Opposite of leeward.

Y

YAW - To swing off course, as when due to the impact of a following or quartering sea.

YAWL - A two-masted sailboat with the small mizzen mast stepped abaft the rudder post.

INDEX

U

V

W

THE UNITED STATES COAST GUARD

What is the United States Coast Guard?

The U.S. Coast Guard is one of five branches of the U.S. Armed Forces, and falls under the jurisdiction of the U.S. Department of Transportation except during wartime when it becomes part of the U.S. Navy. The Coast Guard is the country's oldest continuous sea-going service with responsibilities including search and rescue (SAR), Maritime Law Enforcement (MLE), Aids to Navigation (ATON), Ice Breaking, Environmental Protection, Port Security and Military Readiness. In order to accomplish these missions, the Coast Guard's 41,000 active-duty men and women, 8,000 Reservists, and 35,000 Auxiliarists serve in a variety of job fields ranging from communication specialists and small-boat operators and maintenance specialists to electronic technicians and aviation mechanics. The U.S. Coast Guard, during an average day will:

- board 90 large vessels for port safety checks
- process 120 seaman's documents
- seize 209 pounds of marijuana and 170 pounds of cocaine worth $9.2 million
- conduct 120 law enforcement boardings
- investigate 17 marine accidents
- inspect 64 commercial vessels
- save 14 lives
- assist 328 people in distress
- save $2,490,000 in property
- service 150 aids to navigation
- interdict 176 illegal migrants

What are some benefits of joining?

- A Steady Income
- Career Advancement
- Paid Vacation
- Training
- Free Health Care
- Allowances
- Tax Advantages
- GI Bill
- Tuition Assistance
- Life Insurance
- VA Home Loans
- Exchange & Commissary Privileges
- Survivor Benefits
- Moving Allowances
- Travel

What Should I ask my recruiter?

Coast Guard recruiters must present an accurate picture of Coast Guard training. You should be aware of all aspects of the Coast Guard environment. Be sure you fully understand the enlistment contract. If there are doubts or questions, find out more BEFORE you sign, because an important part of your future is at stake. You should ask about:

- Literature with details and qualifications for each speciality area.
- Films or videos which show training and duties in the Coast Guard.
- How long your basic and technical training is, and where.
- Any special enlistment programs if you have completed Junior ROTC or Sea Cadet training.
- Remote assignments overseas and long duty tours.
- Haircut and grooming standards.
- Chances for off-duty education and educational benefits.
- Any guaranteed training programs.

Where do I get more information?

For More information about our other oppotunities for action, please call 1-800-424-883, or see a United States Coast Guard Recruiter. To talk to a recruiter directly, call 1-800-GET-USCG.

Join the United States Coast Guard Auxiliary

Benefits – Why Join?

- Knowing that you are helping to save lives - Either directly through Search and Rescue Operations or indirectly, through the Auxiliary's Public Education and Courtesy Examination Programs.

- Special Training - the Auxiliary and the Coast Guard provide training on all aspects of boating.

- Fellowship - the auxiliary provides opportunities to meet and have fun with fellow boaters.

- If you enjoy boating, boat with the best.

Eligibility – Who can Join?

- Membership is open to all citizens of the United States and its territories who are at least 17 years old.

- The Auxiliary is looking for members who have at least 25% ownership in a Facility (see below), although individuals with special skills that may be useful (and there are a lot of these) are also welcome.

- New members will need to complete the <u>Boating Safety and Seamanship Course</u>, <u>Sailing and Seamanship Course</u>, or an equivalent test, and then pass an open-book Basic Qualification exam (BQ). Fellow Auxiliarists will help new members with the BQ material, which provides information about the Coast Guard and the Auxiliary, from chain of command, to special training, to proper uniforms.

Auxiliary "Facilities" include:

- Privately owned boats and yachts

- Aircraft

- Land-based or mobile radio equipment

To Find Out More

- Contact your local Auxiliary Flotilla - Look in many marinas or boat supply stores. There is usually information provided by the Auxiliary with local phone numbers

- Contact the closest Director of Auxiliary

- Call the Coast Guard Customer Infoline at: 800-368-5647

UNITED STATES COAST GUARD AUXILIARY

A DAY IN THE LIFE .....

- Educated 929 People on Recreational Boating Safety and Marine Environmental Issues
- Completed 7 Regatta Patrols
- Completed 91 Safety Patrol
- Accomplished 19 SAR Assists
- Saved $729,000.00 Worth of Property
- Assisted 56 People In Trouble On The Water
- Completed 15 Recruiting Support Missions
- Performed 615 Courtesy Marine Examinations
- Participated in 120 USCG Operational Support Missions
- Participated in 42 USCG Administrative Support Missions
- Completed 122 Public Affairs Missions

And, every single day of the year, on average, one or two recreational boaters whose death was certain, sure, and imminent - somewhere on the waters of the United States - had his or her life saved by a member of the U.S. Coast Guard Auxiliary.

> "...GIVE US ONE DAY A MONTH AND WE'LL GIVE YOU AMERICA'S GREAT MARINE SERVICE TEAM WHICH ENHANCES BOATING PLEASURE AND REDUCES BOATING FATALITIES BY PROMOTING BOATING SAFETY NATIONWIDE......"

COURSES OFFERED BY THE AUXILIARY:

- Water 'n Kids Class
- Boats 'n Kids Class
- Personal Water Craft
- Boating Safely
- Boating Skills and Seamanship
- Sailing and Seamanship

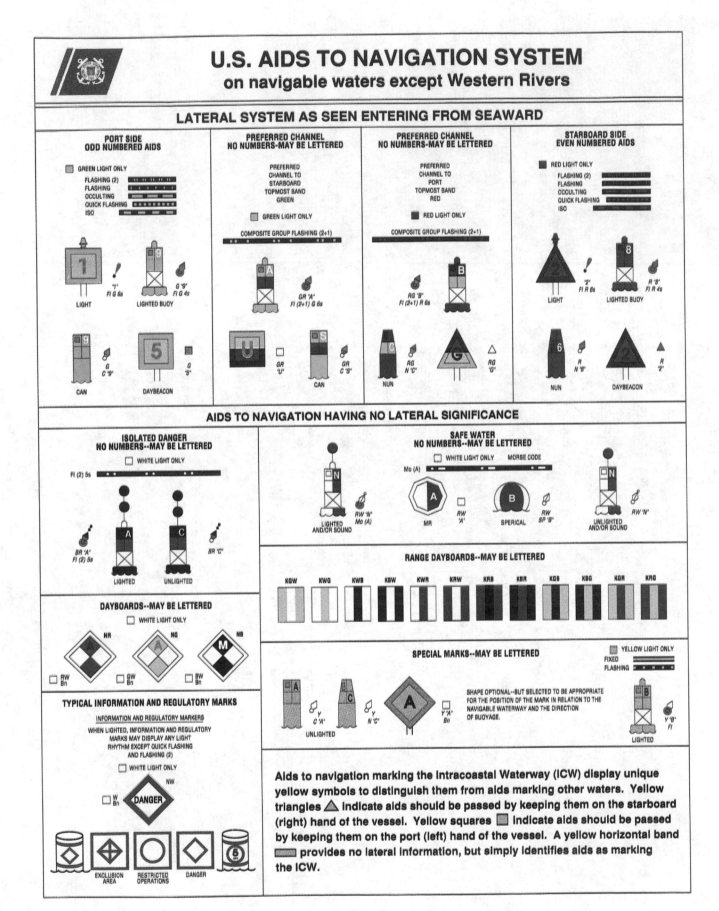

U.S. AIDS TO NAVIGATION SYSTEM
on navigable waters except Western Rivers

Plate 1

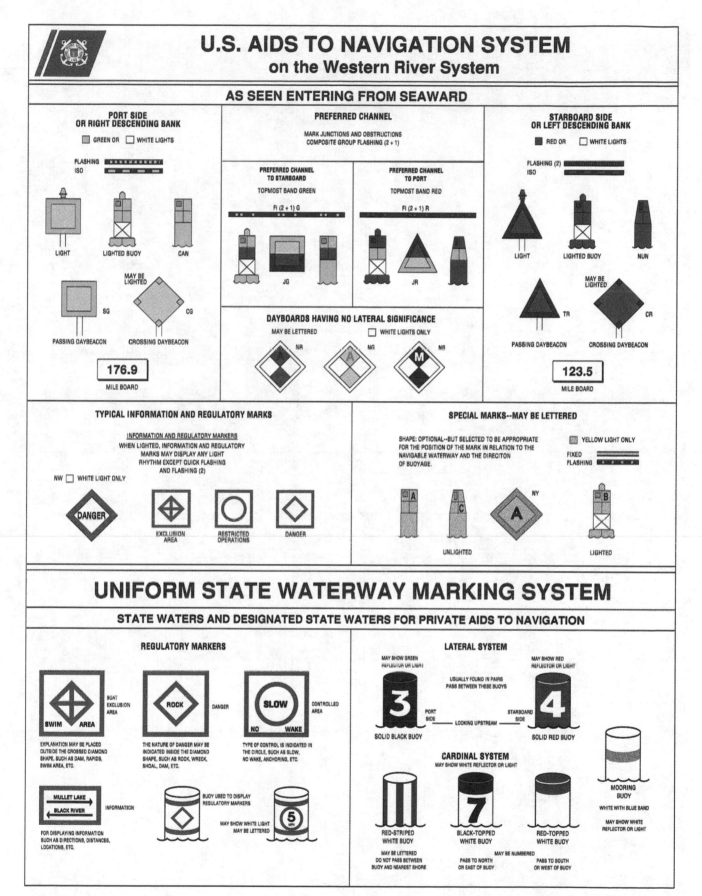

Plate 2